Contents

Ethan's "Hungry Man's Cast Iron" Meatloaf

Prep: 25 mins **Cook:**2 hrs 30 mins **Additional:** 15 mins**Total:** 3 hrs 10 mins **Servings:** 12 **Yield:** 12 servings

Ingredients

- 4 ½ pounds ground beef
- 1 ½ cups Italian bread crumbs
- 2 (4.5 ounce) packages noodle soup mix (such as Lipton Soup Secrets)
- 1 (8 ounce) can tomato sauce (such as Hunt's), divided
- 4 large eggs eggs
- 1 yellow onion, chopped
- ½ cup ketchup
- ½ (4 ounce) packet saltine crackers, crumbled
- 2 tablespoons Worcestershire sauce, divided
- 1 tablespoon barbeque sauce
- 2 teaspoons steak sauce (such as A1)
- 2 teaspoons salt
- 2 teaspoons ground black pepper, divided
- 1 ½ teaspoons garlic powder, divided
- 1 teaspoon onion powder, divided
- ½ teaspoon cayenne pepper

Directions

1. Place a large cast iron skillet in the oven. Preheat oven to 375 degrees F (190 degrees C).
2. Combine ground beef, Italian bread crumbs, noodle soup mix, 1/2 the tomato sauce, eggs, onion, ketchup, cracker crumbs, 1 tablespoon Worcestershire sauce, barbeque sauce, steak sauce, salt, 1 1/2 teaspoons black pepper, 1 teaspoon garlic powder, and 1/2 teaspoon onion powder in a large bowl; mix well.
3. Mix remaining tomato sauce, 1 tablespoon Worcestershire sauce, 1/2 teaspoon black pepper, 1/2 teaspoon garlic powder, 1/2 teaspoon onion powder, and cayenne pepper in a small bowl until topping smooth.
4. Remove skillet from the oven. Place ground beef mixture in skillet, smoothing the top. Spread topping over beef.
5. Bake in the preheated oven until beef is mostly cooked through, about 1 hour 30 minutes. Remove from oven and drain off grease. Return to the oven and continue cooking until meatloaf juices run clear and an instant-read thermometer inserted into the center reads at least 160 degrees F (70 degrees C), about hour more.
6. Remove meatloaf from oven and allow to cool for 15 minutes before serving.

Nutrition Facts

Per Serving:

520.3 calories; protein 36.6g 73% DV; carbohydrates 33g 11% DV; fat 26.2g 40% DV; cholesterol 187.5r 63% DV; sodium 1884mg 75% DV.

Sheila's Peach Cobbler with Pecans

Prep: 15 mins **Cook:** 30 mins**Total:** 45 mins **Servings:** 6 **Yield:** 6 servings

Ingredients

- 3 cups sliced fresh peaches
- 2 teaspoons lemon juice

- 1 ½ cups white sugar
- 1 cup chopped pecans
- 1 teaspoon ground cinnamon
- 1 ½ cups self-rising flour, or as needed
- ½ cup white sugar
- ½ cup brown sugar
- 1 teaspoon ground cinnamon
- ¼ cup butter, melted
- 2 tablespoons butter, cut into small pieces
- 1 tablespoon raw sugar, or as desired

Directions

1. Preheat oven to 400 degrees F (200 degrees C).
2. Stir peaches with lemon juice in a bowl to prevent fruit from browning. Transfer to a cast iron skillet and stir in 1 1/2 cup white sugar, pecans, and 1 teaspoon cinnamon. Bring to a soft boil, stirring often.
3. Whisk self-rising flour, 1/2 cup white sugar, brown sugar, and 1 teaspoon cinnamon in a bowl. Stir melted butter into the mixture (batter should resemble cooked oatmeal). Spoon batter over hot peach filling in the skillet; dot topping with 2 tablespoons of butter pieces and sprinkle with raw sugar.
4. Bake cobbler in the preheated oven until topping is golden brown, about 30 minutes.

Cook's Note:

I used lemon juice because I didn't have citric acid on hand. I baked mine a few minutes, then carefully turned the dough in peach juices 2 or 3 times to wet the flour, then continued to bake until it totaled 30 minutes.

Nutrition Facts

Per Serving:

668 calories; protein 4.9g 10% DV; carbohydrates 110.9g 36% DV; fat 24.9g 38% DV; cholesterol 30.5mg 10% DV; sodium 485.4mg 19% DV.

Zucchini Cornbread

Prep: 15 mins **Cook:** 30 mins**Total:** 45 mins **Servings:** 8 **Yield:** 8 servings

Ingredients

- 1 cup coarsely chopped zucchini
- 1 cup milk
- ½ cup chopped onion
- 2 large eggs eggs
- ¼ cup vegetable oil
- 1 ¼ cups cornmeal
- 1 cup all-purpose flour
- 2 tablespoons white sugar
- 4 teaspoons baking powder
- 1 teaspoon salt
- 1 cup shredded Cheddar cheese

Directions

1. Preheat oven to 400 degrees F (200 degrees C). Grease a 10-inch cast-iron skillet, and place it into the oven while it preheats.
2. Place the zucchini, milk, onion, eggs, and vegetable oil into a blender, and pulse 5 to 8 times, until thoroughly mixed and the zucchini and onion have been chopped into very small pieces.

3. Mix together the cornmeal, flour, sugar, baking powder, and salt in a large bowl. Pour the zucchini mixture into the cornmeal mixture, stirring to combine, and gently mix in the Cheddar cheese.
4. Carefully pour the batter into the hot greased skillet, smooth it out with a spoon, and bake until the cornbread is golden brown and a toothpick inserted into the center comes out clean, about 30 minutes.

Nutrition Facts

Per Serving:

306.7 calories; protein 9.6g 19% DV; carbohydrates 36g 12% DV; fat 13.9g 21% DV; cholesterol 63.8mg 21% DV; sodium 656mg 26% DV.

Southern Biscuits with Mayonnaise

Prep: 15 mins **Cook:** 20 mins **Additional:** 10 mins**Total:** 45 mins **Servings:** 12 **Yield:** 1 dozen biscuits

Ingredients

- ⅔ cup buttermilk
- 2 tablespoons vegetable oil
- 3 tablespoons mayonnaise
- 2 cups self-rising flour

Directions

1. In a large bowl mix together the buttermilk, oil, and mayonnaise. Gradually stir in the flour and mix until all ingredients are combined.
2. Turn dough out onto a well floured surface. If dough is sticky knead in a little extra flour. Pat the dough out to about a 1/2-inch thickness. Use a biscuit cutter to cut dough into pieces. Place into an oiled cast iron skillet. Allow biscuits to rest in the pan for 10 minutes.
3. Bake in a preheated 425 degree F (220 degrees C) until nicely browned, about 20 minutes.

Nutrition Facts

Per Serving:

124.2 calories; protein 2.5g 5% DV; carbohydrates 16.2g 5% DV; fat 5.4g 8% DV; cholesterol 1.9mg 1% DV; sodium 298.5mg 12% DV.

Southern Corn Pone Bread

Prep: 20 mins **Cook:** 25 mins**Total:** 45 mins **Servings:** 8 **Yield:** 1 corn pone cake

Ingredients

- ¼ cup canola oil
- 1 ½ cups white cornmeal
- 1 ½ teaspoons salt
- 1 ⅓ cups buttermilk
- 2 large eggs eggs

Directions

1. Preheat oven to 425 degrees F (220 degrees C). Place a 9 inch cast iron skillet on the center rack.
2. When the skillet is hot, carefully remove the skillet from the oven. Pour the canola oil into the skillet and gently swirl the pan to coat the bottom and the sides. Return the pan to the oven for ten minutes.
3. While the oil is heating, mix together the cornmeal and salt in a medium bowl. Add the eggs and buttermilk and mix together to make a thin batter.
4. Carefully pull out the rack with the cast iron skillet and pour the batter into the preheated skillet.
5. Bake the corn pone until a toothpick inserted into the center comes out clean, 20 to 25 minutes. If desired, turn the oven to broil for the last few minutes of baking to brown the top.
6. Remove the skillet from the oven and shake the pan to loosen the corn pone from the skillet. Serve the corn pone warm from the skillet or turn out onto a plate.

Nutrition Facts
Per Serving:
178.9 calories; protein 4.8g 10% DV; carbohydrates 19.6g 6% DV; fat 9.4g 15% DV; cholesterol 48.1mg
16% DV; sodium 504.4mg 20% DV.

Not-So-Corny Tamale Pie

Prep: 15 mins **Cook:** 25 mins **Total:** 40 mins **Servings:** 8 **Yield:** 8 servings

Ingredients

- 2 teaspoons vegetable oil, or as needed
- 1 small onion, chopped
- 1 ½ pounds ground beef
- 1 (15 ounce) can pinto beans, rinsed and drained
- 1 (15 ounce) can black beans, rinsed and drained
- ½ cup shredded Mexican cheese blend
- 1 (14 ounce) can diced tomatoes with green chile peppers (such as RO*TEL)
- 2 (8.5 ounce) packages corn bread mix (such as Jiffy)
- ⅔ cup milk
- 2 large eggs eggs

Directions

1. Preheat oven to 400 degrees F (200 degrees C).
2. Heat oil in a cast-iron skillet over medium-high heat; saute onion until lightly browned, 5 to 10 minutes. Add ground beef; cook and stir until beef is browned and crumbly, 5 to 10 minutes. Mix pinto beans and black beans into beef mixture.
3. Sprinkle Mexican cheese blend over beef-bean mixture; stir. Mix diced tomatoes with green chile peppers into beef-bean mixture.
4. Mix corn bread mix, milk, and eggs together in a bowl until batter is smooth. Spread batter over top of beef-bean mixture.
5. Bake in the preheated oven until a toothpick inserted in the center of the cornbread comes out clean, 15 to 20 minutes.

Cook's Note:
Bake the pie in a 2-quart baking dish or 9x13-inch baking dish if you don't have a cast-iron skillet.

Nutrition Facts
Per Serving:
571.4 calories; protein 28.4g 57% DV; carbohydrates 58.2g 19% DV; fat 25g 38% DV; cholesterol 109.9mg
37% DV; sodium 1611.4mg 65% DV.

Cast Iron Cornbread

Prep: 10 mins **Cook:** 25 mins **Total:** 35 mins **Servings:** 8 **Yield:** 8 servings

Ingredients

- ½ cup unsalted butter
- 1 cup cornmeal
- ½ teaspoon fine salt
- 1 pinch cayenne pepper
- 3 tablespoons honey, or to taste
- 2 large eggs
- 1 ½ cups buttermilk
- 1 cup self-rising flour

Directions

1. Preheat the oven to 400 degrees F (200 degrees C).
2. Melt butter in a cast iron skillet. Turn off heat and set butter aside until needed.
3. Combine cornmeal, salt, cayenne, honey, eggs, and buttermilk. Whisk to combine. Add flour and 1/2 th butter from the pan; whisk again. Pour batter over the remaining butter in the skillet
4. Bake in the preheated oven until a toothpick inserted into the center comes out clean, about 25 minutes. Let cool briefly before slicing.

Nutrition Facts

Per Serving:

281 calories; protein 6g 12% DV; carbohydrates 34.1g 11% DV; fat 13.6g 21% DV; cholesterol 78.8mg 26% DV; sodium 412.6mg 17% DV.

The RIGHT WAY To Cook Greens!

Prep: 15 mins **Cook:** 5 mins **Total:** 20 mins **Servings:** 4 **Yield:** 4 servings

Ingredients

- ¼ cup bacon drippings
- 4 bunches collard greens, tough stems removed
- 1 pinch salt to taste
- 3 cups water

Directions

1. Heat bacon drippings in a cast-iron skillet over medium heat. Add the greens. Stir-fry, I suppose, since you are stirring and frying, for 1 to 4 minutes (depends on how tough the greens are) or until greens are limp, tender, and have greatly reduced in size. Pork fat is good because it helps cover the bitterness of greens while bringing out their great flavor.
2. At this point, you have a choice. Either serve them straight from the pan with a sprinkling of salt, or add 3 to 4 cups of water and salt to taste, and boil the greens 1 hour for extra tender, probably-won't-even-have-to-chew greens. If you don't have teeth, clearly you see which way to go here.

Cook's Notes

A mess of greens is about as many greens as you can cram into a plastic shopping bag.

To get drippings, fry 4 to 8 strips of bacon in an iron skillet or frying pan until you have gotten most of the grease out and it thickly coats the bottom of the pan.

KEEP IN MIND: If you boil them without frying first, you will have to boil for at least two hours with som type of pork to reduce the bitterness of greens in general. My father boils his all day with a ham hock, and they turn out pretty good, but there is no need for that type of time commitment unless, of course, you have an unbreakable family tradition or sadly have no teeth (no judgement here, toothless ones)!

Nutrition Facts

Per Serving:

217.3 calories; protein 6.9g 14% DV; carbohydrates 15.9g 5% DV; fat 16g 25% DV; cholesterol 14.1mg 5% DV; sodium 83.6mg 3% DV.

Skillet Apple Brownie

Prep: 20 mins **Cook:** 40 mins **Additional:** 20 mins **Total:** 1 hr 20 mins **Servings:** 6 **Yield:** 6 servings

Ingredients

- 1 cup all-purpose flour
- ½ cup white sugar
- ½ cup brown sugar

- ¼ teaspoon salt
- 2 teaspoons ground cinnamon
- 1 teaspoon ground nutmeg
- ½ teaspoon ground cloves
- 2 large eggs eggs, lightly beaten
- 1 teaspoon vanilla extract
- ½ cup melted butter
- 2 cups apples - peeled, cored and chopped
- ½ cup chopped pecans
- 1 tablespoon butter

Directions

1. Preheat an oven to 350 degrees F (175 degrees C). Place an 8- or 9-inch cast iron skillet into the oven to preheat. Whisk together the flour, white sugar, brown sugar, salt, cinnamon, nutmeg, and cloves in a bowl; set aside.
2. Beat together the eggs, vanilla extract, and melted butter in a mixing bowl. Toss the apples and pecans in the flour mixture, then stir into the egg mixture until combined. Melt 1 tablespoon of butter in the preheated skillet, swirling to coat the pan.
3. Pour the batter into the hot pan, and replace into the oven. Bake until the sides are dry and a toothpick inserted into the center of the brownie comes out clean, about 40 minutes. Cool in the skillet 20 minutes before removing and slicing.

Cook's Note

If you don't have a cast iron skillet, you can use a well-greased frying pan or other skillet with the non-metal parts wrapped in a double layer of tinfoil OR just use a regular casserole or brownie pan, just don't preheat glass or ceramic!!! When you add the batter it will shatter.

Nutrition Facts

Per Serving:

478 calories; protein 5.5g 11% DV; carbohydrates 58.8g 19% DV; fat 26g 40% DV; cholesterol 107.8mg 36% DV; sodium 249.4mg 10% DV.

Skillet Chicken Pasta

Prep: 10 mins **Cook:** 25 mins**Total:** 35 mins **Servings:** 2 **Yield:** 2 servings

Ingredients

- ½ (8 ounce) package spaghettini
- 2 tablespoons olive oil
- 8 plum tomato (blank)s roma (plum) tomatoes, halved and sliced
- 1 teaspoon garlic powder
- ½ teaspoon dried oregano
- 2 teaspoons dried basil
- 1 pinch salt
- 1 teaspoon ground black pepper
- 1 ½ teaspoons white sugar
- 1 tablespoon ketchup
- 3 tablespoons olive oil
- 2 eaches skinless, boneless chicken breasts, cut into thin strips
- 2 eaches garlic cloves, crushed
- 1 green bell pepper, chopped
- 1 red bell pepper, chopped

- 1 red onion, chopped
- 1 cup sliced fresh mushrooms
- ¼ cup grated Parmesan cheese

Directions

1. Bring a large pot of water to a boil over high heat. Stir in the spaghettini, and return to a boil. Cook th pasta until it has cooked through, but is still firm to the bite, about 6-8 minutes. Drain well and keep warm.
2. Heat 2 tablespoons oil in a large skillet over medium heat. Stir in the tomatoes; cook until they soften and begin to break down. Stir in the garlic powder, oregano, basil, salt, pepper, sugar, and ketchup. H sauce through and reserve.
3. Heat the remaining 3 tablespoons oil in a separate cast iron skillet over medium heat. Stir in chicken; cook until browned. Stir in crushed garlic cloves; cook for 1 additional minute.
4. Remove chicken from skillet and reserve. Turn heat to high. Stir the green pepper, red pepper, onion, and mushrooms into the skillet and cook until they begin to soften. Stir in browned chicken. Turn hea medium and cook until chicken is no longer pink in the center, and the vegetables are cooked through about 5 minutes.
5. Toss the chicken and vegetables with the tomato sauce and the hot pasta. Serve sprinkled with Parme: cheese.

Nutrition Facts

Per Serving:

767.5 calories; protein 43g 86% DV; carbohydrates 62.4g 20% DV; fat 40.1g 62% DV; cholesterol 74.6n 25% DV; sodium 524.9mg 21% DV.

Skillet Corn Bread

Prep: 10 mins **Cook:** 20 mins **Additional:** 10 mins **Total:** 40 mins **Servings:** 8 **Yield:** 8 servings

Ingredients

- 1 ¼ cups milk
- 1 cup cornmeal
- 1 cup all-purpose flour
- 4 teaspoons baking powder
- ¾ teaspoon kosher salt
- 2 large eggs eggs, beaten
- ¼ cup unsalted butter, melted
- 1 tablespoon vegetable oil

Directions

1. Preheat oven to 425 degrees F (220 degrees C). Place 9-inch cast-iron skillet in oven to warm it.
2. Mix milk and cornmeal together in small bowl and let soak for 10 minutes.
3. Sift flour, baking powder, and salt together in a mixing bowl. Beat cornmeal mixture, eggs, and butter into the flour mixture until you have a smooth batter, about 1 minute.
4. Remove skillet from oven. Swish vegetable oil in the skillet to coat; pour off excess.
5. Pour batter into the skillet.
6. Bake in the preheated oven until a toothpick inserted into the center comes out clean, 18 to 23 minute: Cut into wedges to serve.

Nutrition Facts

Per Serving:

224.6 calories; protein 5.8g 12% DV; carbohydrates 28.1g 9% DV; fat 9.9g 15% DV; cholesterol 64.8mg 22% DV; sodium 459.2mg 18% DV.

Fresh Apple Cake I Wyoming Stew

Prep: 10 mins **Cook:** 1 hr 30 mins**Total:** 1 hr 40 mins **Servings:** 8 **Yield:** 8 servings

Ingredients

- 1 pound cubed beef stew meat
- 2 teaspoons meat tenderizer
- 1 (14.5 ounce) can chicken broth
- 1 (10.75 ounce) can condensed cream of chicken soup
- 1 (1 ounce) envelope dry onion soup mix
- 1 (16 ounce) package frozen stew vegetables
- 1 (10 ounce) can refrigerated crescent dinner rolls

Directions

1. Heat a cast-iron skillet over medium-high heat. Sprinkle meat tenderizer over beef cubes, and cook in the hot skillet until browned. Drain off any excess juice. In a small bowl, mix together the chicken broth, cream of chicken soup and onion soup mix. Pour over the meat, reduce heat to low, and simmer for 45 minutes.
2. Preheat the oven to 350 degrees F (175 degrees C). Add the frozen stew vegetables to the skillet, and simmer for 10 more minutes. Unroll the crescent roll dough, and arrange to cover the top of the pan like a pie.
3. Bake for 10 to 15 minutes in the preheated oven, or until the top is golden brown.
4. Remove from oven and serve.

Nutrition Facts

Per Serving:

389.9 calories; protein 19g 38% DV; carbohydrates 25.9g 8% DV; fat 22g 34% DV; cholesterol 52.9mg 18% DV; sodium 1026.1mg 41% DV.

Ricotta, Bacon, and Arugula Skillet Pizza

Prep: 15 mins **Cook:** 10 mins**Total:** 25 mins **Servings:** 6 **Yield:** 1 pizza

Ingredients

- 3 cups ricotta cheese
- 4 eaches green onions, sliced diagonally
- 3 tablespoons olive oil, divided
- ¼ teaspoon red pepper flakes
- 1 store-bought thin pizza crust
- 5 slices cooked bacon, crumbled, or more to taste
- ½ cup freshly grated Parmesan cheese
- 1 pinch salt and ground black pepper to taste
- 1 bunch fresh arugula
- 1 lemon, juiced

Directions

1. Preheat the oven to 400 degrees F (200 degrees C).
2. Mix ricotta cheese, green onions, 1 tablespoon olive oil, and red pepper flakes together in a bowl. Spread over pizza crust.
3. Heat remaining 2 tablespoons olive oil in a cast iron skillet over medium heat. Place pizza crust with ricotta mixture in the skillet; add bacon and Parmesan cheese and cook the bottom of the pizza, 3 to 4 minutes.

4. Leave pizza in the skillet and place in the preheated oven to bake until top of pizza begins to brown slightly, 7 to 8 minutes. Remove pizza from the oven carefully, top with salt and pepper, arugula, and a drizzle of lemon juice, in that order. Serve warm.

Cook's Notes:

Sliced pepperoncini adds good flavor to the pizza, if that's your style.

You can substitute flatbread for the pizza crust if you want a lighter bite. You can also use a homemade thin crust instead of store-bought, if desired.

Place this pizza on your grill for an even better flavor experience.

Nutrition Facts

Per Serving:

442.6 calories; protein 24.9g 50% DV; carbohydrates 33.1g 11% DV; fat 23.9g 37% DV; cholesterol 52.2mg 17% DV; sodium 831.5mg 33% DV.

Mini Cast Iron Skillet S'mores

Prep: 5 mins **Cook:** 3 mins**Total:** 8 mins **Servings:** 4 **Yield:** 4 s'mores

Ingredients

- 4 cracker (2-1/2" square)s graham cracker squares
- 1 milk chocolate candy bar (such as Hershey's), broken into 4 pieces
- 2 regulars large marshmallows, halved

Directions

1. Set oven rack about 6 inches from the heat source and preheat the oven's broiler.
2. Place 1 graham cracker square in each of 4 miniature cast iron skillets. Top each graham cracker square with 1 piece of chocolate, and 1/2 marshmallow.
3. Place skillets in the preheated oven and cook until marshmallows begin to brown, about 3 minutes.
4. Remove miniature skillets from oven and gently press marshmallows into chocolate with a spatula.

Nutrition Facts

Per Serving:

96.1 calories; protein 1g 2% DV; carbohydrates 14.8g 5% DV; fat 4g 6% DV; cholesterol 2.5mg 1% DV; sodium 51.5mg 2% DV.

Roast Chicken with Croutons and Onions

Prep: 20 mins **Cook:** 1 hr 30 mins **Additional:** 5 mins**Total:** 1 hr 55 mins **Servings:** 6 **Yield:** 1 whole roast chicken

Ingredients

- 1 (4 pound) whole chicken
- 1 tablespoon olive oil, or as needed
- 1 pinch salt and ground black pepper to taste
- 1 large rosemary sprig, leaves stripped and finely chopped
- 1 large white onion, cut into 1-inch chunks
- 2 cups cubed French bread
- 1 large whole rosemary sprig
- ¼ lemon, juiced

Directions

1. Rinse chicken, pat thoroughly dry with paper towels, and allow to reach room temperature.
2. Preheat oven to 390 degrees F (199 degrees C).
3. Rub olive oil over outside of chicken and sprinkle skin and inside of cavity generously with salt. Rub

black pepper and chopped rosemary onto chicken skin. Place 2 or 3 chunks of onion and French bread into cavity, along with whole rosemary sprig. Place chicken into a cast iron skillet and arrange remaining onion and bread chunks around the bird; squeeze lemon juice over the chicken, onion, and bread cubes.

4. Bake in the preheated oven for 30 minutes and turn chicken over so breast side is down. Bake 30 more minutes; turn chicken back over so breast side is up. Bake until chicken is browned and the juices run clear, an additional 30 minutes (90 total minutes roasting time). An instant-read meat thermometer, inserted into the thickest part of a thigh, not touching bone, should read at least 160 degrees F (70 degrees C). Let chicken rest 5 to 10 minutes before slicing chicken meat and serving with onion and bread cubes.

Nutrition Facts
Per Serving:
348.6 calories; protein 44.2g 88% DV; carbohydrates 9.1g 3% DV; fat 13.8g 21% DV; cholesterol 127.6mg 43% DV; sodium 204.6mg 8% DV.

Cascadia Fideua

Prep: 30 mins **Cook:** 55 mins **Total:** 1 hr 25 mins **Servings:** 4 **Yield:** 4 servings

Ingredients
- 3 cups chicken stock, or more if needed
- 2 cloves garlic, minced
- 1 pinch saffron
- 1 cup pancetta bacon, diced
- 2 tablespoons olive oil, divided
- ½ cup diced carrots
- ½ cup frozen artichoke hearts, thawed
- ½ cup fresh green beans
- 2 cups diced white onion
- 1 pinch salt and black pepper to taste
- 2 cups diced tomatoes
- 1 (16 ounce) package spaghetti, broken into 2-inch pieces

Directions
1. Combine the chicken stock, garlic, and saffron in a saucepan. Warm until hot, but not too hot to put your finger in. Cover, and keep warm over low heat so the saffron can infuse while you continue with the recipe.
2. Cook and stir the diced pancetta in a cast iron skillet over medium heat until most of the fat has rendered out and the pancetta has cooked to your desired degree of doneness, about 10 minutes. Once done, remove the pancetta and set aside.
3. Discard the grease and pour in 1 tablespoon of olive oil. Cook and stir the carrots, artichoke hearts, and green beans until the vegetables begin to soften, then remove from the pan and set aside. Heat the remaining 1 tablespoon of olive oil in the skillet, and stir in the onion. Season with salt and pepper, and cook until the onion has softened, about 10 minutes. Add the tomatoes, and cook until the tomato-onion mixture is practically a paste, 15 to 20 minutes.
4. Spread the onion mixture evenly over the bottom of the skillet, and sprinkle evenly with the broken spaghetti pieces. Pour in enough saffron broth to cover the noodles, then arrange the pancetta and cooked vegetables over top. Add additional saffron broth as needed to cover the vegetables. Bring to a simmer, then reduce heat to medium-low, and cook until the noodles are tender, about 15 minutes.

Cook's Note

Paella and fideua are versatile dishes. In fact the original idea was to make this dish and use up leftovers, and rumor has it that paella is an old Arabic word for 'leftovers'. Little trivia for ya! You can make paella with sausage, chicken, scallops, clams, mussels, and all sorts of veggies; ideally they work the same. If you only use vegetables, you can replace the olive oil with butter.

Nutrition Facts

Per Serving:

635.6 calories; protein 23.5g 47% DV; carbohydrates 101g 33% DV; fat 15.5g 24% DV; cholesterol 16.8m 6% DV; sodium 895.1mg 36% DV.

Blueberry Cornmeal Upside-Down Cake

Prep: 30 mins **Cook:** 50 mins **Additional:** 15 mins **Total:** 1 hr 35 mins **Servings:** 16 **Yield:** 2 9-inch cakes

Ingredients

Cake Batter:

- 3 cups all-purpose flour
- 1 ½ cups cornmeal
- 1 tablespoon baking powder
- 1 teaspoon salt
- 1 pound unsalted butter, softened
- 3 cups white sugar
- 8 eaches eggs, at room temperature
- 1 ½ cups sour cream
- 1 tablespoon vanilla extract

Berries:

- ½ cup unsalted butter, divided
- 1 cup brown sugar, divided
- 6 cups fresh blueberries, divided

Directions

1. Preheat the oven to 350 degrees F (175 degrees C).
2. Mix all-purpose flour, cornmeal, baking powder, and salt together in a bowl.
3. Cream together butter and sugar with an electric mixer until smooth. Beat in eggs one at a time, scraping down the bowl after each addition. Add sour cream and vanilla; combine until smooth. Add flour mixture and mix until incorporated. Set aside.
4. Divide butter between two 9-inch cast iron pans; melt over medium-low heat, about 1 minute. Add 1/2 of the brown sugar to each pan; cook until butter and sugar begin to bubble, 2 to 3 minutes. Divide blueberries between the two pans and remove from stove top.
5. Divide cornmeal batter between the pans; place each on a sheet pan.
6. Bake in the preheated oven until a toothpick inserted into the middle comes out clean, 45 to 50 minutes.
7. Let cool slightly, about 15 minutes. Run a knife around the outer edges of each cake and invert onto a cutting board for slicing.

Nutrition Facts

Per Serving:

696.2 calories; protein 7.5g 15% DV; carbohydrates 88.4g 29% DV; fat 36.1g 56% DV; cholesterol 167.6mg 56% DV; sodium 260.3mg 10% DV.

Skillet-Roasted Tilapia with Green Beans

Prep: 15 mins **Cook:** 15 mins **Total:** 30 mins **Servings:** 4 **Yield:** 4 servings

Ingredients

- 1 pound fresh green beans, trimmed

- 2 tablespoons butter, melted, divided
- 1 teaspoon salt, divided
- ½ teaspoon ground black pepper
- 4 (5 ounce) fillets tilapia
- ½ cup unseasoned bread crumbs
- ¼ cup sliced almonds, coarsely chopped
- 1 tablespoon finely chopped fresh sage

Directions

1. Place a large cast iron skillet in the oven. Preheat the oven to 450 degrees F (230 degrees C).
2. Toss green beans, 1/2 tablespoon butter, 1/2 teaspoon salt, and 1/4 teaspoon pepper in the hot skillet. Return to the oven and roast for 3 minutes.
3. Meanwhile, sprinkle remaining 1/2 teaspoon salt and 1/4 teaspoon pepper over tilapia fillets.
4. Combine bread crumbs, almonds, and sage in a small bowl; stir in remaining 1 1/2 tablespoon butter. Sprinkle enough topping over the tilapia to cover the surface. Press topping lightly to adhere.
5. Carefully remove skillet from the oven. Sprinkle remaining topping over the green beans and toss lightly. Place the tilapia on top, in the center of the skillet.
6. Roast until flesh flakes easily with a fork, 10 to 13 minutes.

Nutrition Facts

Per Serving:

317.9 calories; protein 34.3g 69% DV; carbohydrates 19.2g 6% DV; fat 11.5g 18% DV; cholesterol 67.3mg 22% DV; sodium 791.2mg 32% DV.

Cast Iron Skillet Peach Custard

Prep: 15 mins **Cook:** 45 mins **Total:** 1 hr **Servings:** 8 **Yield:** 1 10-inch skillet

Ingredients

- 1 tablespoon margarine, or as needed
- 2 cups white sugar
- 2 eaches eggs
- 2 ¼ cups pureed peaches
- 2 cups all-purpose baking mix (such as Bisquick)
- 1 teaspoon vanilla extract

Directions

1. Preheat the oven to 350 degrees F (175 degrees C). Grease a 10-inch cast iron skillet with margarine.
2. Combine sugar and eggs in a large bowl; beat with an electric mixer until creamy. Mix in pureed peaches and baking mix until combined. Add vanilla extract and stir until well blended. Pour into the prepared skillet.
3. Bake in the preheated oven until top is golden brown, 45 to 55 minutes.

Cook's Note:

If you like a wetter pudding, use canned peaches (instead of fresh) and use all the juice from the can. Add this juice after you add all the other blended ingredients to the skillet.

Nutrition Facts

Per Serving:

354.1 calories; protein 3.5g 7% DV; carbohydrates 70.8g 23% DV; fat 7g 11% DV; cholesterol 40.9mg 14% DV; sodium 410.3mg 16% DV.

Sweet Potato and Ham Hash

Total Time: **Prep**: 20 min **Cook**: 20 min. **Makes** :4 servings

Ingredients

- 2 cups cubed peeled sweet potatoes
- 2 tablespoons butter
- 1 tablespoon olive oil
- 1 medium onion, chopped
- 1 small sweet red pepper, chopped
- 3 green onions, chopped
- 1 red chili pepper, seeded and finely chopped
- 3 garlic cloves, minced
- 2 cups cubed fully cooked ham
- 1/2 teaspoon pepper
- 1/4 teaspoon salt
- 4 eggs
- 1/4 cup shredded white cheddar cheese

Directions

1. In a large skillet, saute sweet potatoes in butter and oil until crisp-tender. Add the onion, red pepper, green onions and chili pepper. Saute 4-5 minutes longer or until tender. Add garlic; cook 1 minute longer. Stir in the ham, pepper and salt.
2. With the back of a spoon, make four wells in the potato mixture; add an egg to each well. Sprinkle with cheese. Cover and cook for 4-5 minutes or until egg whites are completely set.

Nutrition Facts

1 serving: 379 calories, 22g fat (9g saturated fat), 271mg cholesterol, 1237mg sodium, 23g carbohydrate (7 sugars, 4g fiber), 23g protein.

Turkey Biscuit Stew

Total Time: **Prep**: 15 min **Bake**: 20 min. **Makes** :8 servings

Ingredients

- 1/3 cup chopped onion
- 1/4 cup butter, cubed
- 1/3 cup all-purpose flour
- 1/2 teaspoon salt
- 1/8 teaspoon pepper
- 1 can (10-1/2 ounces) condensed chicken broth, undiluted
- 3/4 cup 2% milk
- 2 cups cubed cooked turkey
- 1 cup cooked peas
- 1 cup cooked whole baby carrots
- 1 tube (16.3 ounces) large refrigerated buttermilk biscuits

Directions

1. In a 10-in. ovenproof skillet, saute onion in butter until tender. Stir in the flour, salt and pepper until blended. Gradually add broth and milk. Bring to a boil. Cook and stir until thickened and bubbly, about 2 minutes. Add the turkey, peas and carrots; heat through. Separate biscuits and arrange over the stew.
2. Bake at 375° until biscuits are golden brown, 20-25 minutes.

Nutrition Facts

3/4 cup stew with 1 biscuit: 345 calories, 15g fat (7g saturated fat), 53mg cholesterol, 960mg sodium, 36g carbohydrate (7g sugars, 2g fiber), 18g protein.

Kaiserschmarren

Total Time: **Prep**: 15 min **Bake**: 20 min.**Makes** :8 servings

Ingredients

- 2 cups all-purpose flour
- 1 cup whole milk
- Pinch salt
- 4 large eggs, separated
- 1/4 cup unsalted butter, melted
- 1/4 cup sugar
- 1/2 cup butter
- 1/2 cup raisins
- 2 tablespoons confectioners' sugar
- Stewed plums or other fruit

Directions

1. Mix flour and milk to a thick paste. Add salt. Stir in egg yolks and unsalted butter. Beat egg whites with 1/4 cup sugar until stiff and fold into batter.
2. Melt 1/2 cup butter in a 12-in. round cast-iron skillet or 11x7-in. glass baking dish. Pour in batter. Scatter raisins over top. Bake at 375° for 20 minutes.
3. Using two forks, tear pancake into pieces and allow to steam for a moment. Dust with confectioners' sugar and serve with plums or other fruit.

Nutrition Facts

1 serving: 379 calories, 21g fat (12g saturated fat), 156mg cholesterol, 183mg sodium, 41g carbohydrate (16g sugars, 1g fiber), 8g protein.

Skillet-Grilled Catfish

Total Time:Prep/Total time: 25 min**Makes** :4 servings

Ingredients

- 1/4 cup all-purpose flour
- 1/4 cup cornmeal
- 1 teaspoon onion powder
- 1 teaspoon dried basil
- 1/2 teaspoon garlic salt
- 1/2 teaspoon dried thyme
- 1/4 to 1/2 teaspoon white pepper
- 1/4 to 1/2 teaspoon cayenne pepper
- 1/4 to 1/2 teaspoon pepper
- 4 catfish fillets (6 to 8 ounces each)
- 1/4 cup butter

Directions

1. In a large shallow dish, combine the first 9 ingredients. Add catfish, one fillet at a time, and turn to coat.
2. Place a large cast-iron skillet on a grill rack over medium-high heat. Melt butter in the skillet; add catfish in batches, if necessary. Grill, covered, until fish just begins to flake easily with a fork, 5-10 minutes on each side.

Nutrition Facts

1 fillet: 222 calories, 15g fat (8g saturated fat), 51mg cholesterol, 366mg sodium, 14g carbohydrate (0 sugars, 1g fiber), 8g protein.

Butternut Squash Rolls

Total Time: Prep: 30 min + rising   **Bake**: 20 min. **Makes :2 dozen**

Ingredients

- 1 package (1/4 ounce) active dry yeast
- 1 cup warm 2% milk (110° to 115°)
- 1/4 cup warm water (110° to 115°)
- 3 tablespoons butter, softened
- 2 teaspoons salt
- 1/2 cup sugar
- 1 cup mashed cooked butternut squash
- 5 to 5-1/2 cups all-purpose flour, divided

Directions

1. In a large bowl, dissolve yeast in milk and water. Add the butter, salt, sugar, squash and 3 cups flour; beat until smooth. Add enough remaining flour to form a soft dough.
2. Turn onto a floured surface; knead until smooth and elastic, 6-8 minutes. Place in a greased bowl, turning once to grease top. Cover and let rise in a warm place until doubled, about 1 hour.
3. Punch dough down. Form into rolls; place in 2 greased 10-in. cast-iron skillets or 9-in. round baking pans. Cover and let rise until doubled, about 30 minutes.
4. Bake at 375° for 20-25 minutes or until golden brown.

Nutrition Facts

1 roll: 135 calories, 2g fat (1g saturated fat), 5mg cholesterol, 213mg sodium, 26g carbohydrate (5g sugars 1g fiber), 3g protein.

Creamy Salmon Linguine

Total Time:Prep/Total time: 25 min**Makes :5** servings

Ingredients

- 8 ounces uncooked linguine
- 1 bunch broccoli, cut into florets
- 2 tablespoons butter
- 2 garlic cloves, minced
- 2 cups heavy whipping cream
- 2 tablespoons lemon juice
- 1 pound fully cooked salmon, flaked
- 1/4 teaspoon salt
- 1/4 teaspoon pepper
- 1 cup shredded Parmesan cheese
- 3 tablespoons minced fresh basil or 1 tablespoon dried basil
- 2 tablespoons capers, drained
- 2 teaspoons grated lemon zest

Directions

1. Cook linguine according to package directions, adding broccoli during the last 5 minutes of cooking.
2. Meanwhile, in a large skillet, heat butter over medium heat. Add garlic; cook and stir 1 minute. Stir in cream and lemon juice. Bring to a boil. Reduce heat; simmer, uncovered, 2-3 minutes or until slightly

thickened, stirring constantly.

3. Add salmon, salt and pepper; heat through. Drain linguine and broccoli; add to skillet. Stir in cheese, basil, capers and lemon zest.

Nutrition Facts

1-1/3 cups: 802 calories, 55g fat (30g saturated fat), 207mg cholesterol, 649mg sodium, 44g carbohydrate (4g sugars, 6g fiber), 36g protein.

Deep-Dish Sausage Pizza

Total Time: **Prep**: 30 min + rising   **Bake**: 30 min. + standing**Makes :8 slices**

Ingredients

- 1 package (1/4 ounce) active dry yeast
- 2/3 cup warm water (110° to 115°)
- 1-3/4 to 2 cups all-purpose flour
- 1/4 cup vegetable oil
- 1 teaspoon each dried oregano, basil and marjoram
- 1/2 teaspoon garlic salt
- 1/2 teaspoon onion salt

TOPPINGS:

- 4 cups shredded part-skim mozzarella cheese, divided
- 2 medium green peppers, chopped
- 1 large onion, chopped
- 1/2 teaspoon each dried oregano, basil and marjoram
- 1 tablespoon olive oil
- 1 cup grated Parmesan cheese
- 1 pound bulk pork sausage, cooked and drained
- 1 can (28 ounces) diced tomatoes, well drained
- 2 ounces sliced pepperoni

Directions

1. In a large bowl, dissolve yeast in warm water. Add 1 cup flour, oil and crust seasonings; beat until smooth. Add enough remaining flour to form a soft dough.
2. Turn onto a floured surface; knead until smooth and elastic, 6-8 minutes. Place in a greased bowl; turn once to grease top. Cover and let rise in a warm place until doubled, about 1 hour.
3. Punch dough down; roll out into a 15-in. circle. Transfer to a well-greased 12-in. heavy ovenproof skillet or round baking pan, letting crust drape over edges. Sprinkle with 1 cup mozzarella.
4. In a skillet, saute the green peppers, onion and topping seasonings in oil until tender; drain. Layer half the mixture over crust. Layer with half the Parmesan, sausage and tomatoes. Sprinkle with 2 cups mozzarella. Repeat layers. Fold crust over to form an edge.
5. Bake at 400° for 20 minutes. Sprinkle with pepperoni and remaining mozzarella. Bake until crust is browned, 10-15 minutes longer. Let stand for 10 minutes before slicing.

Nutrition Facts

1 slice: 548 calories, 34g fat (14g saturated fat), 68mg cholesterol, 1135mg sodium, 32g carbohydrate (8g sugars, 4g fiber), 27g protein.

Servings: 8 **Yield:** 1 cast iron skillet

Ingredients

- 1 cup white sugar

- ⅓ cup butter
- 1 egg
- 1 ½ cups all-purpose flour
- 1 teaspoon baking soda
- 1 pinch salt
- 1 ½ teaspoons ground cinnamon
- 1 ½ teaspoons vanilla extract
- 2 cups apple - peeled, cored, and chopped
- ½ cup chopped walnuts

Directions
1. Preheat oven to 350 degrees F (175 degrees C). Grease a 9 inch cast iron skillet. In a medium bowl, mix the flour, baking soda, salt and cinnamon together and set aside.
2. In a large bowl, cream the butter and sugar until fluffy. Add the egg and beat well. Add the vanilla. Add the flour mixture and beat well. Fold in the chopped apples and nuts.
3. Pour batter into a greased 9 inch cast iron skillet or cake pan. Bake at 350 degrees F (175 degrees C) for 45 minutes, or until a toothpick inserted into the cake comes out clean.

Nutrition Facts
Per Serving:
326.3 calories; protein 4.5g 9% DV; carbohydrates 48.7g 16% DV; fat 13.4g 21% DV; cholesterol 43.6mg 15% DV; sodium 221.6mg 9% DV.

Grandma's Pineapple Upside-Down Cake
Prep: 15 mins **Cook:** 30 mins **Total:** 45 mins **Servings:** 8 **Yield:** 8 servings

Ingredients
- ⅓ cup butter
- ½ cup brown sugar, packed
- 8 piece (blank)s pineapple rings
- 8 halves pecan halves
- 1 cup all-purpose flour
- 1 teaspoon baking powder
- ¼ teaspoon salt
- ⅔ cup white sugar
- 2 large eggs eggs
- ¼ cup pineapple juice

Directions
1. Preheat oven to 350 degrees F (175 degrees C).
2. Melt butter in a 9-inch cast iron skillet over medium heat. Stir in brown sugar; heat until bubbly. Remove from heat. Arrange pineapple rings and pecans on top.
3. Sift flour, baking powder, and salt together in a bowl; repeat sifting twice more.
4. Beat white sugar and eggs together in a bowl with an electric mixer until light and fluffy.
5. Alternate folding flour mixture and pineapple juice into the egg mixture in 3 batches, beginning and ending with the flour mixture. Pour over pineapple slices.
6. Bake in the preheated oven until a toothpick inserted into the center comes out clean, 30 to 35 minutes. Let cool in the skillet for 5 minutes. Invert carefully onto a serving platter.

Nutrition Facts
Per Serving:

319.3 calories; protein 3.4g 7% DV; carbohydrates 55.1g 18% DV; fat 10.2g 16% DV; cholesterol 66.8mg 22% DV; sodium 214.9mg 9% DV.

Real Southern Cornbread

Prep: 10 mins **Cook:** 50 mins**Total:** 1 hr **Servings:** 12 **Yield:** 12 servings

Ingredients

- 2 cups cornmeal
- 2 cups all-purpose flour
- ½ teaspoon salt
- 2 tablespoons baking powder
- 2 large eggs eggs
- 1 cup margarine, melted
- 4 cups buttermilk
- ¼ cup corn oil

Directions

1. In a large bowl mix together the corn meal, flour, salt, and baking powder.
2. In a separate bowl mix together the eggs, butter, and buttermilk. Add to the dry ingredients and stir until well blended.
3. Heat a dry 12 inch cast iron skillet over high heat for 2 minutes. Add corn oil to skillet, swirl oil around to coat bottom and sides. Leave remaining oil in pan. Return to high heat for 1 minute.
4. Pour the cornbread batter into the skillet and cook on high heat until bubbles start to form in the center. Remove from stove.
5. Bake in a preheated 400 degree F (200 degree C) oven for 40 to 50 minutes, or until a knife inserted into the center comes out clean. Serve warm.

Nutrition Facts
Per Serving:
369.4 calories; protein 7.7g 15% DV; carbohydrates 36.3g 12% DV; fat 22g 34% DV; cholesterol 34.3mg 11% DV; sodium 620.9mg 25% DV.

Perfect Crispy Fried Chicken

Prep: 20 mins **Cook:** 30 mins **Additional:** 12 hrs 20 mins**Total:** 13 hrs 10 mins **Servings:** 3 **Yield:** 3 servings

Ingredients

- 3 medium (blank)s chicken leg quarters, cut into thighs and drumsticks
- 2 cups buttermilk, or as needed to cover
- ¾ cup all-purpose flour
- ¼ cup cornmeal
- 1 teaspoon granulated onion
- 1 teaspoon granulated garlic
- 1 teaspoon ground thyme
- 1 tablespoon salt
- ½ teaspoon paprika
- ¼ teaspoon monosodium glutamate (MSG)
- ¼ teaspoon baking powder
- ⅛ teaspoon cayenne pepper
- 4 large egg whites egg whites, beaten until foamy
- 2 cups vegetable oil for frying

Directions

1. Place chicken drumsticks and thighs in a bowl and pour enough buttermilk over chicken to cover. Cove and refrigerate for 12 to 24 hours.
2. Combine flour, cornmeal, granulated onion, granulated garlic, thyme, salt, paprika, monosodium glutamate, baking powder, and cayenne pepper in a large, wide bowl.
3. Remove chicken from buttermilk and shake off excess. Discard buttermilk. Pat chicken dry with paper towels.
4. Dip chicken into egg whites and press into flour mixture. Allow coated chicken to rest on a wire rack fc 20 to 30 minutes.
5. Fill a cast-iron skillet or deep fryer with vegetable oil about 1/3 full. Heat to 350 degrees F (175 degree C).
6. Preheat oven to 250 degrees F (120 degrees C).
7. Fry chicken in hot oil in batches until golden brown and no longer pink in the center, 8 to 10 minutes p side. Thighs may take longer to fry than drumsticks. Transfer fried chicken to a wire rack or a paper towel-lined tray to drain. Keep chicken warm in preheated oven while frying remaining pieces.

Nutrition Facts

Per Serving:

766.7 calories; protein 55.4g 111% DV; carbohydrates 46.6g 15% DV; fat 38.7g 60% DV; cholesterol 149.4mg 50% DV; sodium 2788.8mg 112% DV.

Mom's Sweet Buttermilk Corn Bread

Prep: 10 mins **Cook:** 25 mins **Total:** 35 mins **Servings:** 10 **Yield:** 10 servings

Ingredients

- ¼ cup vegetable oil
- 2 cups white cornmeal
- ¾ cup all-purpose flour
- ⅓ cup white sugar
- 4 ½ teaspoons baking powder
- ½ teaspoon baking soda
- 1 teaspoon salt
- 2 large eggs eggs
- 2 cups buttermilk

Directions

1. Preheat oven to 450 degrees F (230 degrees C).
2. Pour vegetable oil into a 10-inch cast-iron skillet and swirl oil to coat bottom and sides of skillet. Place skillet into preheated oven until very hot, 3 to 5 minutes. Remove skillet from oven.
3. Whisk cornmeal, flour, sugar, baking powder, baking soda, and salt in a bowl. Beat eggs in a separate bowl and stir buttermilk into eggs. Pour half (2 tablespoons) of vegetable oil from the hot skillet into buttermilk mixture, retaining remaining oil in skillet, and beat until oil is incorporated. Mix buttermilk mixture into dry ingredients to make a smooth batter. Pour batter into skillet.
4. Bake in the oven until top is golden brown, 18 to 20 minutes. Cut cornbread into servings while in skillet; serve warm.

Nutrition Facts

Per Serving:

231.4 calories; protein 5.8g 12% DV; carbohydrates 35.6g 12% DV; fat 7.8g 12% DV; cholesterol 39.2m 13% DV; sodium 589.1mg 24% DV.

Oven-Baked Beef Tagliata

Prep: 20 mins **Cook:** 20 mins **Additional:** 10 mins**Total:** 50 mins **Servings:** 6 **Yield:** 6 servings

Ingredients

- 3 large cloves garlic, minced
- 2 teaspoons finely chopped fresh rosemary
- 1 teaspoon chopped fresh oregano
- 1 tablespoon sea salt, divided
- 2 teaspoons ground black pepper, divided
- 2 (1 1/2) pounds sirloin steaks, about 1 1/2-inches thick
- 1 tablespoon extra-virgin olive oil
- 6 cups loosely packed arugula
- 2 teaspoons extra virgin olive oil
- 1 teaspoon lemon juice
- ¼ lemon, sliced
- 2 ounces Parmesan cheese, shaved

Directions

1. Place a cast-iron skillet in the oven and preheat the oven to 350 degrees F (175 degrees C).
2. Combine garlic, rosemary, oregano, 1 1/2 teaspoons salt, and 1/2 teaspoon pepper in a small bowl. Rub spice mixture all over the steaks.
3. Remove the skillet from the oven and add 1 tablespoon oil. Add steak and return to the preheated oven. Cook until steaks is browned on both sides, turning after 10 minutes, about 20 minutes total.
4. Transfer steak to a cutting board and let rest for 10 minutes; then slice.
5. Spread arugula on a platter and top with steak slices. Drizzle with 2 teaspoons olive oil and lemon juice and top with Parmesan cheese.

Nutrition Facts

Per Serving:

333.3 calories; protein 45.5g 91% DV; carbohydrates 3g 1% DV; fat 14.5g 22% DV; cholesterol 86.3mg 29% DV; sodium 1116.9mg 45% DV.

Mrs. Patti's Mexican Cornbread

Prep: 15 mins **Cook:** 45 mins**Total:** 1 hr **Servings:** 8 **Yield:** 8 servings

Ingredients

- 1 ½ cups yellow cornmeal
- 1 tablespoon baking powder
- 1 teaspoon salt
- 1 cup sour cream
- 2 large eggs eggs
- 1 (14 ounce) can cream-style corn
- 1 onion, chopped
- ⅔ cup vegetable oil
- ¼ cup chopped jalapeno peppers, or to taste
- 3 cups shredded Cheddar cheese, divided

Directions

1. Preheat oven to 400 degrees F (200 degrees C). Grease a large cast-iron skillet.
2. Whisk cornmeal, baking powder, and salt in a bowl; beat sour cream and eggs into cornmeal mixture

until thoroughly combined. Stir cream-style corn, onion, vegetable oil, and jalapeno peppers into batter.

3. Pour half the batter into prepared cast-iron skillet; spread 1 cup Cheddar cheese over batter. Pour in remaining batter and spread remaining 2 cups Cheddar cheese on top.
4. Bake in the preheated oven until set and the cheese topping is melted and browned, about 45 minutes.

Nutrition Facts

Per Serving:

555.1 calories; protein 16.1g 32% DV; carbohydrates 34.6g 11% DV; fat 40.2g 62% DV; cholesterol 103.6mg 35% DV; sodium 913.8mg 37% DV.

The Best Corn Bread You'll Ever Eat

Prep: 5 mins **Cook:** 30 mins**Total:** 35 mins **Servings:** 8 **Yield:** 6 to 8 servings

Ingredients

- 1 egg
- 1 ⅓ cups milk
- ¼ cup vegetable oil
- 2 cups self-rising corn meal mix
- 1 (8 ounce) can cream-style corn
- 1 cup sour cream

Directions

1. Heat oven to 425 degrees F (220 degrees C). Grease a 9 inch iron skillet.
2. In a large bowl, beat the egg. Add milk, oil, sour cream, cream corn, and cornmeal mix; stir until cornmeal is just dampened. Pour batter into greased skillet.
3. Bake for 25 to 30 minutes, or until knife inserted in center comes out clean.

Nutrition Facts

Per Serving:

327.6 calories; protein 6.4g 13% DV; carbohydrates 40.8g 13% DV; fat 15.9g 24% DV; cholesterol 39.2m 13% DV; sodium 772.1mg 31% DV.

Basic Buttermilk Corn Bread

Prep: 10 mins **Cook:** 25 mins **Total:** 35 mins **Servings:** 8 **Yield:** 8 servings

Ingredients

- 2 cups cornmeal
- 1 ½ cups buttermilk
- ¼ cup vegetable oil
- 1 egg
- 2 tablespoons butter

Directions

1. Preheat oven to 400 degrees F (200 degrees C). Whisk together the cornmeal, buttermilk, vegetable oi and egg in a bowl to form a batter.
2. Melt the butter in a cast-iron skillet over medium heat, and swirl the melted butter all over the bottom and up the sides of the skillet. Let the butter heat until it gives off a faint toasted fragrance; pour the batter into the hot skillet.
3. Place the skillet into the preheated oven, and bake until golden brown, 25 to 30 minutes.

Nutrition Facts

Per Serving:

240.3 calories; protein 4.8g 10% DV; carbohydrates 29.6g 10% DV; fat 11.3g 17% DV; cholesterol 32.7m 11% DV; sodium 79.8mg 3% DV.

Old Fashioned Caramel Pie

Prep: 25 mins **Additional:** 4 hrs **Total:** 4 hrs 25 mins **Servings:** 8 **Yield:** 1 - 9 inch pie

Ingredients

- 1 (9 inch) pie shell, baked
- 1 cup white sugar
- ⅓ cup all-purpose flour
- ⅛ teaspoon salt
- 2 cups milk
- 4 large egg yolks egg yolks, beaten
- 1 cup white sugar

Directions

1. In a medium saucepan, mix together 1 cup sugar, flour, salt, milk, and egg yolks, stirring until smooth. Cook over medium heat until thick and bubbly, stirring constantly. Remove from heat and set aside.
2. Sprinkle remaining 1 cup sugar in a 10 inch cast iron skillet. Cook over medium heat, stirring constantly until sugar is caramelized. Remove from heat and carefully pour into warm cream mixture. Stir until smooth. Pour mixture into pastry. Chill completely and serve with whipped cream

Nutrition Facts
Per Serving:

387.8 calories; protein 5.3g 11% DV; carbohydrates 67.8g 22% DV; fat 11.2g 17% DV; cholesterol 107.3mg 36% DV; sodium 187.4mg 8% DV.

Maple-Pear Tarte Tatin

Prep: 15 mins **Cook:** 30 mins **Additional:** 5 mins**Total:** 50 mins **Servings:** 8 **Yield:** 1 9-inch tart

Ingredients

- ½ (17.3 ounce) package frozen puff pastry, thawed
- ¼ cup butter
- ⅓ cup brown sugar
- ¼ teaspoon ground cinnamon
- 1 pinch ground nutmeg
- ¼ cup maple syrup
- 4 medium pear (approx 2-1/2 per lb)s firm pears - peeled, cored, and halved, or more as needed

Directions

1. Preheat oven to 375 degrees F (190 degrees C).
2. Roll puff pastry out on a lightly floured surface to 1/4-inch thickness; place in the refrigerator.
3. Melt butter in a 9-inch cast iron skillet over medium heat; stir in brown sugar, cinnamon, and nutmeg and cook and stir until sugar dissolves, about 5 minutes. Stir maple syrup into brown sugar mixture; cook, stirring, until mixture begins to bubble. Remove skillet from heat.
4. Place one pear half, cut side up, into the center of skillet. Cut remaining pear halves in half again; arrange pear quarters around the center pear, cut sides up.
5. Place skillet over medium-low heat; cook pears, basting with syrup mixture, until they begin to soften, about 5 minutes. Remove skillet from heat.
6. Remove puff pastry from refrigerator; place pastry over pears, tucking edges of pastry around pears inside skillet.

7. Bake in the preheated oven until pastry is puffed and golden, about 20 minutes; allow to cool for 5 minutes. Place a serving plate over skillet; invert to remove tart (skillet will still be hot). Serve warm.

Nutrition Facts
Per Serving:
329.3 calories; protein 2.6g 5% DV; carbohydrates 42.4g 14% DV; fat 17.6g 27% DV; cholesterol 15.3mg 5% DV; sodium 121.5mg 5% DV.

Loaded Chocolate Chip Skillet Cookie

Prep: 15 mins **Cook:** 35 mins **Additional:** 15 mins**Total:** 1 hr 5 mins **Servings:** 12 **Yield:** 1 10-inch skille cookie

Ingredients
- 1 ½ cups all-purpose flour
- ½ cup rolled oats
- 1 teaspoon baking soda
- 1 teaspoon ground cinnamon
- ½ teaspoon salt
- 10 tablespoons white sugar
- ½ cup butter, softened
- ½ cup packed light brown sugar
- ¼ cup shortening
- 2 eaches eggs
- 1 teaspoon vanilla extract
- 1 (12 ounce) bag semisweet chocolate chips
- ½ cup chopped pecans

Directions
1. Preheat the oven to 350 degrees F (175 degrees C).
2. Whisk flour, oats, baking soda, cinnamon, and salt together in a medium bowl.
3. Cream white sugar, butter, brown sugar, and shortening in the bowl of a stand mixer until light and fluffy, 3 to 5 minutes. Add eggs, 1 at a time, mixing after each addition until fully incorporated. Mix in vanilla extract. Gradually mix in dry ingredients until combined. Stir in chocolate chips and pecans.
4. Transfer dough to a well seasoned 10-inch cast iron skillet. Press down with your fingers to distribute evenly over the bottom of the skillet.
5. Bake in the preheated oven until top is firm to the touch and edges have started to pull away from the sides of the skillet, 35 to 40 minutes.
6. Remove from the oven and let cool for about 15 to 20 minutes. Run a spatula around the edges, lifting the cookie slightly as you go around. Carefully invert cookie onto a cutting board and then invert again onto a serving platter.

Nutrition Facts
Per Serving:
427.9 calories; protein 4.7g 9% DV; carbohydrates 52.2g 17% DV; fat 24.7g 38% DV; cholesterol 47.6mg 16% DV; sodium 272.7mg 11% DV.

Screaming Potatoes

Servings: 4 **Yield:** 4 servings

Ingredients
- 2 pounds clean, scrubbed new red potatoes
- 1 tablespoon kosher salt
- 2 tablespoons water

Directions

1. Place the potatoes in the bottom of a large cast iron skillet. Place about 2 tablespoons of water in the bottom of the pot and sprinkle with the salt. Cover tightly and place over low heat. Cook for 40-50 minutes. Do not lift the lid during this time. Occasionally give the pan a shake.

Nutrition Facts

Per Serving:

164.1 calories; protein 4.2g 9% DV; carbohydrates 36.1g 12% DV; fat 0.3g; cholesterolmg; sodium 1455mg 58% DV.

Uncle Bill's Hot Water Cornbread

Prep: 10 mins **Cook:** 15 mins **Total:** 25 mins **Servings:** 4 **Yield:** 4 servings

Ingredients

- 3 tablespoons oil
- 1 cup water
- 1 cup yellow cornmeal
- 1 dash seasoned salt

Directions

1. Heat oil in a cast iron skillet over medium heat. Bring water to a boil in a saucepan.
2. Place cornmeal in a bowl. Slowly pour boiling water into the cornmeal; stir until smooth. Mix seasoned salt into the batter.
3. Drop batter with a spoon into the hot oil. Fry until edges are brown, about 5 minutes; flip over bread. Flatten with spatula; fry until bread is cooked through and edges are brown, about 5 minutes. Drain on a paper towel.

Nutrition Facts

Per Serving:

217.9 calories; protein 2.5g 5% DV; carbohydrates 27.4g 9% DV; fat 10.8g 17% DV; cholesterolmg; sodium 61.5mg 3% DV.

Irish Spicy Cornbread

Prep: 10 mins **Cook:** 20 mins **Total:** 30 mins **Servings:** 10 **Yield:** 1 12-inch skillet

Ingredients

- 2 cups all-purpose flour
- 1 cup yellow cornmeal
- ⅓ cup white sugar
- 4 ½ teaspoons baking powder
- 1 ½ teaspoons salt
- 1 ½ teaspoons cayenne pepper
- ½ cup shortening
- 1 ½ cups milk
- 2 large eggs eggs, beaten
- 4 ½ teaspoons hot pepper sauce

Directions

1. Preheat oven and skillet to 400 degrees F (200 degrees C).
2. In a large bowl, mix together flour, cornmeal, sugar, baking powder, salt, and cayenne pepper. Cut in shortening until the mixture resembles coarse bread crumbs. In a small bowl, beat together milk, eggs and hot pepper sauce. Stir milk mixture into the flour/cornmeal mixture until just blended. Remove hot

skillet from oven, spray with non-stick cooking spray and pour batter into skillet.

3. Bake in preheated oven for 20 to 25 minutes, or until a toothpick inserted into center of loaf comes out clean.

Cook's Note:

I use formed cast iron pans that have 5 small corn cob shapes in them, but any cast iron frying pan will do. Heat the pan in the oven before adding mixture and spray well with non-stick spray. With my pans it takes about 18 minutes but for a full loaf in a frying pan it will probably take longer.

Nutrition Facts

Per Serving:

286.4 calories; protein 6.1g 12% DV; carbohydrates 37.7g 12% DV; fat 12.7g 20% DV; cholesterol 40.1m 13% DV; sodium 615.5mg 25% DV.

Single Skillet Hearty Breakfast Deconstructed Pear Pork Chops

Total Time:Prep/Total time: 30 min**Makes :**4 servings

Ingredients

- 1 package (6 ounces) cornbread stuffing mix
- 4 boneless pork loin chops (6 ounces each)
- 1/2 teaspoon pepper
- 1/4 teaspoon salt
- 2 tablespoons butter
- 2 medium pears, chopped
- 1 medium sweet red pepper, chopped
- 2 green onions, thinly sliced

Directions

1. Prepare stuffing mix according to package directions. Meanwhile, sprinkle chops with pepper and salt. In a large skillet, brown pork chops in butter. Sprinkle with pears and red pepper.
2. Top with stuffing and onions. Cook, uncovered, over medium heat until a thermometer inserted in por reads 145°, 8-10 minutes.

Nutrition Facts

1 pork chop with 3/4 cup stuffing mixture: 603 calories, 28g fat (14g saturated fat), 127mgcholesterol, 1094mg sodium, 47g carbohydrate (14g sugars, 5g fiber), 38g protein.

Homemade Sage Sausage Patties

Total Time: Prep 10 min. + chilling **Cook:** 15 min.**Makes :8 servings**

Ingredients

- 1 pound ground pork
- 3/4 cup shredded cheddar cheese
- 1/4 cup buttermilk
- 1 tablespoon finely chopped onion
- 2 teaspoons rubbed sage
- 3/4 teaspoon salt
- 3/4 teaspoon pepper
- 1/8 teaspoon garlic powder
- 1/8 teaspoon dried oregano

Directions

1. In a bowl, combine all ingredients, mixing lightly but thoroughly. Shape into eight 1/2-in.-thick patties. Refrigerate 1 hour.
2. In a large cast-iron or other heavy skillet, cook patties over medium heat until a thermometer reads 160°, 6-8 minutes on each side.

Nutrition Facts

1 patty: 162 calories, 11g fat (5g saturated fat), 49mg cholesterol, 323mg sodium, 1g carbohydrate (0 sugars, 0 fiber), 13g protein.

Pinwheel Steak Potpie

Total Time: **Prep**: 20 min **Bake**: 25 min. **Makes** :6 servings

Ingredients

- 2 tablespoons butter
- 1-1/4 pounds beef top sirloin steak, cut into 1/2-inch cubes
- 1/4 teaspoon pepper
- 1 package (16 ounces) frozen vegetables for stew
- 2 tablespoons water
- 1/2 teaspoon dried thyme
- 1 jar (12 ounces) mushroom or beef gravy
- 1 tube (8 ounces) refrigerated crescent rolls

Directions

1. Preheat oven to 375°. In a 10-in. cast-iron or other ovenproof skillet, heat butter over medium-high heat. Brown beef in batches; remove from pan. Sprinkle with pepper; keep warm.
2. In same skillet, combine vegetables, water and thyme; stir in gravy. Bring to a boil. Reduce heat; simmer, uncovered, until vegetables are thawed. Stir in beef; remove from heat.
3. Unroll crescent dough and separate into 8 triangles. Starting from the wide end of each triangle, roll up a third of the length and place over beef mixture with pointed ends toward the center.
4. Bake, uncovered, until golden brown, 16-18 minutes.

Nutrition Facts

1 piece: 365 calories, 18g fat (6g saturated fat), 67mg cholesterol, 716mg sodium, 29g carbohydrate (4g sugars, 1g fiber), 22g protein.

Chicken Cacciatore

Total Time: **Prep**: 15 min **Cook**: 1-1/2 hours. **Makes** :6 servings

Ingredients

- 1 broiler/fryer chicken (3-1/2 to 4 pounds), cut up
- 1/4 cup all-purpose flour
- Salt and pepper to taste
- 2 tablespoons olive oil
- 2 tablespoons butter
- 1 large onion, chopped
- 2 celery ribs, sliced
- 1 large green pepper, cut into strips
- 1/2 pound sliced fresh mushrooms
- 1 can (28 ounces) tomatoes, drained and chopped
- 1 can (8 ounces) tomato sauce
- 1 can (6 ounces) tomato paste

- 1 cup dry red wine or water
- 1 teaspoon dried thyme
- 1 teaspoon dried rosemary, crushed
- 1 teaspoon dried oregano
- 1 teaspoon dried basil
- 3 garlic cloves, minced
- 1 tablespoon sugar
- Hot cooked pasta
- Grated Parmesan cheese

Directions

1. Dust chicken with flour. Season with salt and pepper. In a large skillet, brown chicken on all sides in oi
   and butter over medium-high heat. Remove chicken to platter.
2. In the same skillet, cook and stir the onion, celery, pepper and mushrooms for 5 minutes. Stir in the
   tomatoes, tomato sauce, tomato paste, wine, herbs, garlic and sugar. Bring to a boil. Reduce heat; cove
   and simmer for 30 minutes.
3. Return chicken to skillet. Cover and simmer for 45-60 minutes or until chicken is tender. Serve over
   pasta and sprinkle with Parmesan cheese.
4. Freeze option: Cool chicken mixture. Freeze in freezer containers. To use, partially thaw in refrigerato
   overnight. Heat through slowly in a covered skillet until a thermometer inserted in chicken reads 165°,
   stirring occasionally.

Nutrition Facts

4-1/2 ounce-weight: 517 calories, 25g fat (8g saturated fat), 112mg cholesterol, 790mg sodium, 28g
carbohydrate (13g sugars, 6g fiber), 39g protein.

Caramel-Apple Skillet Buckle

Total Time: Prep: 35 min **Bake**: 1 hour + standing**Makes :12 servings**

Ingredients

- 1/2 cup butter, softened
- 3/4 cup sugar
- 2 large eggs, room temperature
- 1 teaspoon vanilla extract
- 2 cups all-purpose flour
- 2-1/2 teaspoons baking powder
- 1-3/4 teaspoons ground cinnamon
- 1/2 teaspoon ground ginger
- 1/4 teaspoon salt
- 1-1/2 cups buttermilk
- 2/3 cup packed brown sugar
- 1/2 cup all-purpose flour
- 1/4 cup cold butter
- 3/4 cup finely chopped pecans
- 1/2 cup old-fashioned oats
- 6 cups thinly sliced peeled Gala or other sweet apples (about 6 medium)
- 18 caramels, unwrapped
- 1 tablespoon buttermilk
- Optional toppings: Vanilla ice cream, whipped cream, additional chopped pecans and ground cinnam

Directions

1. Preheat oven to 350°. In a large bowl, cream butter and sugar until light and fluffy, 5-7 minutes. Add eggs, 1 at a time, beating well after each addition. Beat in vanilla. In another bowl, whisk flour, baking powder, cinnamon, ginger and salt; add to creamed mixture alternately with buttermilk, beating well after each addition. Pour into a greased 12-in. cast-iron or other ovenproof skillet.
2. For topping, in a small bowl, mix brown sugar and flour; cut in butter until crumbly. Stir in pecans and oats; sprinkle over batter. Top with apples. Bake until apples are golden brown, 60-70 minutes. Cool in pan on a wire rack.
3. In a microwave, melt caramels with buttermilk; stir until smooth. Drizzle over cake. Let stand until set. Serve with toppings as desired.

Nutrition Facts

1 slice: 462 calories, 19g fat (9g saturated fat), 64mg cholesterol, 354mg sodium, 68g carbohydrate (42g sugars, 3g fiber), 7g protein.

Chicken Bulgur Skillet

Total Time: **Prep**: 15 min **Cook**: 30 min **Makes** :4 servings

Ingredients

- 1 pound boneless skinless chicken breasts, cut into 1-inch cubes
- 2 teaspoons olive oil
- 2 medium carrots, chopped
- 2/3 cup chopped onion
- 3 tablespoons chopped walnuts
- 1/2 teaspoon caraway seeds
- 1/4 teaspoon ground cumin
- 1-1/2 cups bulgur
- 2 cups reduced-sodium chicken broth
- 2 tablespoons raisins
- 1/4 teaspoon salt
- 1/8 teaspoon ground cinnamon

Directions

1. In a large cast-iron or other heavy skillet, cook chicken in oil over medium-high heat until meat is no longer pink. Remove and keep warm. In the same skillet, cook and stir the carrots, onion, nuts, caraway seeds and cumin until onion starts to brown, 3-4 minutes.
2. Stir in bulgur. Gradually add broth; bring to a boil over medium heat. Reduce heat; add the raisins, salt, cinnamon and chicken. Cover and simmer until bulgur is tender, 12-15 minutes.

Nutrition Facts

1-1/2 cups: 412 calories, 8g fat (1g saturated fat), 66mg cholesterol, 561mg sodium, 51g carbohydrate (8g sugars, 12g fiber), 36g protein.

Rustic Honey Cake

Total Time: **Prep**: 15 min   **Bake**: 30 min.+ cooling **Makes** : 12 servings

Ingredients

- 1/2 cup butter, softened
- 1 cup honey
- 2 large eggs, room temperature
- 1/2 cup plain yogurt

- 1 teaspoon vanilla extract
- 2 cups all-purpose flour
- 2 teaspoons baking powder
- 1/2 teaspoon salt
- Assorted fresh fruit and additional honey
- Chopped pistachios, optional

Directions

1. Preheat oven to 350°. Grease a 9-in. cast-iron skillet.
2. In a large bowl, beat butter and honey until blended. Add eggs, 1 at a time, beating well after each addition. Beat in yogurt and vanilla. In another bowl, whisk flour, baking powder and salt; add to butter mixture. Transfer batter to prepared skillet.
3. Bake until a toothpick inserted in center comes out clean, 30-35 minutes. Cool completely in pan on a wire rack. Serve with fruit, additional honey and, if desired, chopped pistachios.
4. Freeze option: Securely wrap cooled cake in foil; freeze. To use, thaw at room temperature and top as directed.

Test Kitchen tips

1. The beauty of this cake is how delicious it is all on its own, but we do recognize that some folks just can't imagine having a cake without frosting. If you're in that camp, just spread some cream cheese frosting on the cooled cake.

Nutrition Facts

1 slice: 248 calories, 9g fat (5g saturated fat), 53mg cholesterol, 257mg sodium, 40g carbohydrate (24g sugars, 1g fiber), 4g protein.

Maple Glazed Pork Chops

Total Time:Prep/Total time: 25 min   **Makes** : 4 servings

Ingredients

- 1/2 cup all-purpose flour
- Salt and pepper to taste
- 4 bone-in pork loin chops (7 ounces each)
- 2 tablespoons butter
- 1/4 cup cider vinegar
- 1/3 cup maple syrup
- 1 tablespoon cornstarch
- 3 tablespoons water
- 2/3 cup packed brown sugar

Directions

1. In a large shallow dish, combine the flour, salt and pepper. Add pork chops and turn to coat. In a large ovenproof skillet, cook chops in butter over medium heat until a thermometer reads 145°, 4-5 minutes on each side. Remove and keep warm.
2. Meanwhile, in the same skillet, bring the vinegar to a boil. Reduce heat; add maple syrup. Cover and cook for 10 minutes. Combine cornstarch and water until smooth; gradually add to maple mixture. Bring to a boil; cook and stir until thickened, about 2 minutes.
3. Place chops on a broiler pan; sprinkle with brown sugar. Broil 4 in. from the heat until sugar is melted 1-2 minutes. Drizzle with maple glaze.

Nutrition Facts

1 pork chop equals 530 calories, 14 g fat (7 g saturated fat), 101 mg cholesterol, 121 mg sodium, 68 g

carbohydrate, trace fiber, 32 g protein.

Parmesan-Bacon Bubble Bread

Total Time: **Prep**: 20 min + rising   **Bake**: 20 min   **Makes :16 servings**

Ingredients

- 1 loaf frozen bread dough, thawed (16 ounces)
- 1/4 cup butter, melted
- 3/4 cup shredded Parmesan cheese
- 6 bacon strips, cooked and finely crumbled, divided
- 1/3 cup finely chopped green onions, divided
- 2 tablespoons grated Parmesan cheese
- 2 tablespoons salt-free herb seasoning blend
- 1-1/2 teaspoons sugar
- Alfredo sauce or marinara sauce, optional

Directions

1. Turn dough onto a lightly floured surface; divide and shape into 16 rolls. Place butter in a shallow bowl. In a large bowl, combine the shredded Parmesan, half the bacon, half the green onions, grated Parmesan, seasoning blend and sugar. Dip dough pieces in melted butter, then toss with cheese mixture to coat. Stack pieces in a greased 9-in. cast-iron skillet.
2. Cover with a kitchen towel; let rise in a warm place until almost doubled, about 45 minutes. Preheat oven to 350°. Bake until golden brown, 20-25 minutes. Top with remaining bacon and green onions. Serve warm and, if desired, with Alfredo or marinara sauce.

Test Kitchen tips

1. Serve with pesto, marinara or Alfredo dipping sauces ... or set out all three and let guests choose their favorite!
2. Cut into slices and fry for a savory French toast breakfast.
3. You can also bake the dough in a greased 9x5-in. loaf pan

Nutrition Facts

1 piece: 140 calories, 6g fat (3g saturated fat), 14mg cholesterol, 311mg sodium, 14g carbohydrate (2g sugars, 1g fiber), 6g protein.

Southwestern Spaghetti

Total Time:Prep/Total time: 30 min   **Makes :5 servings**

Ingredients

- 3/4 pound lean ground beef (90% lean)
- 2-1/4 cups water
- 1 can (15 ounces) tomato sauce
- 2 teaspoons chili powder
- 1/2 teaspoon garlic powder
- 1/2 teaspoon ground cumin
- 1/8 teaspoon salt
- 1 package (7 ounces) thin spaghetti, broken into thirds
- 1 pound zucchini (about 4 small), cut into chunks
- 1/2 cup shredded cheddar cheese

Directions

1. In a large skillet, cook beef over medium heat until no longer pink; drain. Remove beef and set aside. In the same skillet, combine the water, tomato sauce, chili powder, garlic powder, cumin and salt; bring to

a boil. Stir in spaghetti; return to a boil.
Boil for 6 minutes.

2. Add the zucchini. Cook 4-5 minutes longer or until spaghetti and zucchini are tender, stirring several times. Stir in beef and heat through. Sprinkle with cheese.

Nutrition Facts

1 cup: 340 calories, 11g fat (5g saturated fat), 54mg cholesterol, 600mg sodium, 38g carbohydrate (5g sugars, 4g fiber), 24g protein. Diabetic Exchanges: 2 starch, 2 lean meat, 2 vegetable, 1/2 fat.

Beef & Pepper Skillet

Total Time:Prep/Total time: 30 min   **Makes :**5 servings

Ingredients

- 1 pound lean ground beef (90% lean)
- 1 can (14-1/2 ounces) diced tomatoes with mild green chilies, undrained
- 1 can (14-1/2 ounces) beef broth
- 1 tablespoon chili powder
- 1/4 teaspoon salt
- 1/8 teaspoon garlic powder
- 2 cups instant brown rice
- 1 medium sweet red pepper, sliced
- 1 medium green pepper, sliced
- 1 cup shredded Colby-Monterey Jack cheese

Directions

1. In a large cast-iron or other heavy skillet, cook beef over medium heat until no longer pink,6-8 minutes, breaking into crumbles; drain.
2. Add tomatoes, broth, chili powder, salt and garlic powder; bring to a boil. Stir in rice and peppers. Reduce heat; simmer, covered, until liquid is absorbed, 8-10 minutes. Remove from heat; sprinkle with cheese. Let stand, covered, until cheese is melted.
   Freeze option: Before adding cheese, cool beef mixture. Freeze beef mixture and cheese separately in freezer containers. To use, partially thaw in refrigerator overnight. Heat through in a saucepan, stirring occasionally; add a little broth if necessary. Sprinkle with cheese.

Nutrition Facts

1-1/3 cups: 340 calories, 13g fat (7g saturated fat), 64mg cholesterol, 807mg sodium, 31g carbohydrate (5 sugars, 4g fiber), 23g protein.

Traditional Funnel Cakes

Total Time:Prep: **15 min** Cook: **5 min/batch**   Makes: **8 servings**

Ingredients

- 2 cups 2% milk
- 3 large eggs
- 1/4 cup sugar
- 2 cups all-purpose flour
- 2 teaspoons baking powder
- Oil for deep-fat frying
- Confectioners' sugar
- Lingonberry jam or red currant jelly

Directions

1. In a large bowl, combine the milk, eggs and sugar. Combine flour and baking powder; beat into egg mixture until smooth.
2. In a cast-iron or electric skillet, heat 2 inches oil to 375°. Cover the bottom of a funnel spout with your finger; ladle 1/2 cup batter into funnel. Holding the funnel several inches above the skillet, release your finger and move the funnel in a spiral motion until all the batter is released. Scrape funnel with a rubber spatula if needed.
3. Fry until golden brown, 1 minute on each side. Drain on paper towels. Repeat with remaining batter. Dust with confectioners' sugar. Serve warm with jam.

Test Kitchen tips

To pour batter easily into hot oil, simply use a liquid measuring cup or a turkey baster.

Nutrition Facts

1 funnel cake: 300 calories, 15g fat (2g saturated fat), 84mg cholesterol, 157mg sodium, 33g carbohydrate (10g sugars, 1g fiber), 8g protein.

Enchilada Chicken

Total Time Prep: **15min.** Bake: **20 min**. Makes **4 servings**

Ingredients

- 4 boneless skinless chicken breast halves (6 ounces each)
- 2 teaspoons salt-free Southwest chipotle seasoning blend
- 1 tablespoon olive oil
- 1/4 cup enchilada sauce
- 1/2 cup shredded sharp cheddar cheese
- 2 tablespoons minced fresh cilantro

Directions

1. Sprinkle chicken with seasoning blend. In an ovenproof skillet, brown chicken in oil. Top with enchilada sauce, cheese and cilantro. Bake at 350° for 18-20 minutes or until a thermometer reads 170°.

Nutrition Facts

1 chicken breast half : 265 calories, 11g fat (5g saturated fat), 109mg cholesterol, 252mg sodium, 2g carbohydrate (0 sugars, 0 fiber), 38g protein. Diabetic Exchanges: 5 lean meat, 1 fat.

Saucy Beef with Broccoli

Total Time:Prep/Total time: 30 min   **Makes** :2 servings

Ingredients

- 1 tablespoon cornstarch
- 1/2 cup reduced-sodium beef broth
- 1/4 cup sherry or additional beef broth
- 2 tablespoons reduced-sodium soy sauce
- 1 tablespoon brown sugar
- 1 garlic clove, minced
- 1 teaspoon minced fresh gingerroot
- 2 teaspoons canola oil, divided
- 1/2 pound beef top sirloin steak, cut into 1/4-inch-thick strips
- 2 cups fresh small broccoli florets
- 8 green onions, cut into 1-inch pieces

Directions

1. Mix the first 7 ingredients. In a large nonstick skillet, heat 1 teaspoon oil over medium-high heat; stir-fry

beef until browned, 1-3 minutes. Remove from pan.

2. Stir-fry broccoli in remaining oil until crisp-tender, 3-5 minutes. Add green onions; cook just until tender, 1-2 minutes. Stir cornstarch mixture and add to pan. Bring to a boil; cook and stir until sauce is thickened, 2-3 minutes. Add beef and heat through.

Nutrition Facts

1-1/4 cups: 313 calories, 11g fat (3g saturated fat), 68mg cholesterol, 816mg sodium, 20g carbohydrate (11 sugars, 4g fiber), 29g protein. Diabetic Exchanges: 3 lean meat, 1 starch, 1 vegetable, 1 fat.

Confetti Kielbasa Skillet

Total Time:Prep/Total time: 30 min   **Makes :**4 servings

Ingredients

- 1 tablespoon canola oil
- 7 ounces smoked turkey kielbasa, cut into 1/4-inch slices
- 1 medium onion, halved and sliced
- 1/2 cup sliced baby portobello mushrooms
- 2 garlic cloves, minced
- 1/2 cup reduced-sodium chicken broth
- 3/4 teaspoon Mrs. Dash Garlic & Herb seasoning blend
- 1 can (15 ounces) no-salt-added black beans, rinsed and drained
- 1 package (8.8 ounces) ready-to-serve brown rice
- 1 cup frozen corn
- 1/2 cup chopped roasted sweet red peppers
- 4 teaspoons minced fresh cilantro

Directions

1. In a large skillet, heat oil over medium-high heat. Add kielbasa, onion and mushrooms; cook and stir 4 minutes or until vegetables are tender. Add garlic; cook 1 minute longer.
2. Add broth and seasoning blend, stirring to loosen browned bits from pan. Bring to a boil; cook 2-3 minutes or until liquid is almost evaporated. Stir in remaining ingredients; heat through.

Nutrition Facts

1-1/4 cups: 347 calories, 9g fat (1g saturated fat), 31mg cholesterol, 692mg sodium, 45g carbohydrate (4g sugars, 7g fiber), 18g protein. **Diabetic Exchanges:** 3 starch, 2 lean meat, 1/2 fat.

Skillet-Roasted Lemon Chicken with Potatoes

Total Time: Prep: 20 min **Bake**: 25 min.   **Makes :**4 servings

Ingredients

- 1 tablespoon olive oil, divided
- 1 medium lemon, thinly sliced
- 4 garlic cloves, minced and divided
- 1/4 teaspoon grated lemon zest
- 1/2 teaspoon salt, divided
- 1/4 teaspoon pepper, divided
- 8 boneless skinless chicken thighs (4 ounces each)
- 1/4 teaspoon dried rosemary, crushed
- 1 pound fingerling potatoes, halved lengthwise
- 8 cherry tomatoes
- Minced fresh parsley, optional

Directions

1. Preheat oven to 450°. Grease a 10-inch cast-iron or other ovenproof skillet with 1 teaspoon oil. Arrange lemon slices in a single layer in skillet.
2. Combine 1 teaspoon oil, 2 minced garlic cloves, lemon zest, 1/4 teaspoon salt and 1/8 teaspoon pepper; rub over chicken. Place over lemon.
3. In a large bowl, combine rosemary and the remaining oil, garlic, salt and pepper. Add potatoes and tomatoes; toss to coat. Arrange over chicken. Bake, uncovered, 25-30 minutes or until chicken is no longer pink and potatoes are tender. If desired, sprinkle with minced parsley before serving.

Nutrition Facts

2 chicken thighs with 4 ounces potatoes and 2 tomatoes: 446 calories, 20g fat (5g saturated fat), 151mg cholesterol, 429mg sodium, 18g carbohydrate (2g sugars, 3g fiber), 45g protein.

Peach Praline Upside-Down Cake

Total Time: **Prep**: 25 min   **Bake**: 25 min.+ cooling   **Makes :8 servings**

Ingredients

- 4 large eggs, separated
- 1/4 cup butter, cubed
- 2/3 cup packed brown sugar
- 1 teaspoon ground cinnamon
- 1/2 teaspoon ground ginger
- 3 medium peaches, peeled and sliced (2 cups)
- 1/2 cup chopped pecans
- 1 cup cake flour
- 1 teaspoon baking powder
- 1/4 teaspoon salt
- 1 cup sugar
- 1/4 cup 2% milk
- 2 tablespoons butter, melted
- 1 teaspoon vanilla extract
- Whipped cream and toasted pecan halves, optional

Directions

1. Place egg whites in a large bowl; let stand at room temperature 30 minutes. Meanwhile, preheat oven to 375°.
2. In a 10-in. cast-iron or other ovenproof skillet, melt butter over medium heat. Stir in brown sugar, cinnamon and ginger. Remove from heat. Arrange peaches in a single layer over brown sugar mixture; sprinkle with chopped pecans.
3. In a small bowl, whisk flour, baking powder and salt. In a large bowl, beat egg yolks until slightly thickened. Gradually add sugar, beating on high speed until thick and lemon-colored. Beat in milk, melted butter and vanilla. Fold in flour mixture.
4. With clean beaters, beat egg whites on medium until stiff but not dry; gradually fold into batter. Pour batter into skillet. Bake until a toothpick inserted in center comes out clean, 22-27 minutes.
5. Cool 10 minutes before inverting onto a serving plate. If desired, serve warm with whipped cream and pecan halves.

Nutrition Facts

1 slice: 417 calories, 16g fat (7g saturated fat), 117mg cholesterol, 247mg sodium, 64g carbohydrate (48g sugars, 2g fiber), 6g protein.

Easy Beef Taco Skillet

Total Time:Prep/Total time: 20 min   **Makes** :6 servings

Ingredients

- 1 pound ground beef
- 1 small red onion, chopped
- 1 can (15-1/4 ounces) whole kernel corn, drained
- 10 corn tortillas (6 inches), cut into 1-inch pieces
- 1 bottle (8 ounces) taco sauce
- 1-1/4 cups shredded cheddar cheese, divided
- Hot pepper sauce, optional

Directions

1. In a large skillet, cook beef and onion over medium heat until meat is no longer pink; drain. Add the corn, tortillas, taco sauce and 1 cup cheese; heat through. Sprinkle with remaining cheese. Serve with pepper sauce if desired.

Nutrition Facts

1 cup: 415 calories, 19g fat (9g saturated fat), 82mg cholesterol, 705mg sodium, 34g carbohydrate (6g sugars, 4g fiber), 25g protein.

Basil-Butter Steaks with Roasted Potatoes

Total Time:Prep/Total time: 30 min   **Makes** :6 servings

Ingredients

- 1 package (15 ounces) frozen Parmesan and roasted garlic red potato wedges
- 4 beef tenderloin steaks (1-1/4 inches thick and 6 ounces each)
- 1/2 teaspoon salt
- 1/2 teaspoon pepper
- 5 tablespoons butter, divided
- 2 cups grape tomatoes
- 1 tablespoon minced fresh basil

Directions

1. Bake potato wedges according to package directions.
2. Meanwhile, sprinkle steaks with salt and pepper. In a 10-in. cast-iron or other ovenproof skillet, brown steaks in 2 tablespoons butter. Add tomatoes to skillet. Bake, uncovered, at 425° until meat reaches desired doneness, 15-20 minutes (for medium-rare, a thermometer should read 135°; medium, 140°; medium-well, 145°).
3. In a small bowl, combine basil and remaining butter. Spoon over steaks and serve with potatoes.

Nutrition Facts

1 serving: 538 calories, 29g fat (13g saturated fat), 112mg cholesterol, 740mg sodium, 27g carbohydrate sugars, 3g fiber), 41g protein.

Cheese & Mushroom Skillet Pizza

Total Time:Prep/Total time: 30 min   **Makes** :4 slices

Ingredients

- 1 cup all-purpose flour
- 2 teaspoons baking powder
- 1 teaspoon dried oregano

- 1/2 teaspoon salt
- 6 tablespoons water
- 2 tablespoons plus 1 teaspoon olive oil, divided
- 1/2 cup pizza sauce
- 25 slices pepperoni
- 1 jar (4-1/2 ounces) sliced mushrooms, drained
- 1 can (2-1/4 ounces) sliced ripe olives, drained
- 1 cup shredded part-skim mozzarella cheese

Directions

1. Preheat broiler. In a small bowl, whisk flour, baking powder, oregano and salt. Stir in water and 2 tablespoons oil to form a soft dough. Turn onto a floured surface; knead 6-8 times. Roll into a 12-in. circle.
2. Brush bottom of a 12-in. ovenproof skillet with remaining oil; place over medium-high heat. Transfer crust to pan; cook 2-3 minutes on each side or until golden brown. Remove from heat. Spread with pizza sauce; top with pepperoni, mushrooms, olives and cheese.
3. Broil 3-4 in. from heat 3-5 minutes or until cheese is melted.

Nutrition Facts

1 slice: 374 calories, 22g fat (7g saturated fat), 30mg cholesterol, 1284mg sodium, 31g carbohydrate (3g sugars, 3g fiber), 14g protein.

Fudge Brownie Pie

Total Time: **Prep**: 15 min **Bake**: 25 min. **Makes** :6 servings

Ingredients

- 1 cup sugar
- 1/2 cup butter, melted
- 2 large eggs, room temperature
- 1 teaspoon vanilla extract
- 1/2 cup all-purpose flour
- 1/3 cup baking cocoa
- 1/4 teaspoon salt
- 1/2 cup chopped pecans
- Whipped cream, optional
- Strawberries, optional

Directions

1. In a large bowl, beat sugar and butter. Add eggs and vanilla; mix well. Add flour, cocoa and salt. Stir in nuts.
2. Pour into a greased 9-in. pie pan or ovenproof skillet. Bake at 350° until almost set, 25-30 minutes. Serve with whipped cream and strawberries if desired.

Nutrition Facts

1 piece: 409 calories, 24g fat (11g saturated fat), 112mg cholesterol, 274mg sodium, 46g carbohydrate (33g sugars, 2g fiber), 5g protein.

Blackened Halibut

Total Time:**Prep/Total time**: 25 min   **Makes** :4 servings

Ingredients

- 2 tablespoons garlic powder

- 1 tablespoon salt
- 1 tablespoon onion powder
- 1 tablespoon dried oregano
- 1 tablespoon dried thyme
- 1 tablespoon cayenne pepper
- 1 tablespoon pepper
- 2-1/2 teaspoons paprika
- 4 halibut fillets (4 ounces each)
- 2 tablespoons butter

Directions
1. In a large shallow dish, combine the first 8 ingredients. Add fillets, 2 at a time, and turn to coat.
2. In a large cast-iron skillet, cook fillets in butter over medium heat until fish flakes easily with a fork, 3-4 minutes on each side.

Nutrition Facts
1 fillet: 189 calories, 8g fat (4g saturated fat), 51mg cholesterol, 758mg sodium, 3g carbohydrate (1g sugar, 1g fiber), 24g protein. **Diabetic Exchanges:** 3 lean meat, 1 fat.

Milk Cake

Total Time: **Prep**: 20 min **Bake**: 30 min. **Makes** :8 servings

Ingredients
- 1/2 cup whole milk
- 3/4 cup all-purpose flour
- 1 teaspoon baking powder
- 1/4 teaspoon salt
- 3 large eggs, room temperature
- 1 teaspoon vanilla extract
- 1 cup sugar

TOPPING:
- 1/3 cup packed brown sugar
- 1/2 cup chopped pecans
- 2 tablespoons butter, softened
- 2 tablespoons whole milk
- 1 cup sweetened shredded coconut

Directions
1. Scald milk by bringing it almost to a boil; set aside to cool. Combine flour, baking powder and salt; set aside. In a bowl, beat eggs until thick and lemon-colored; stir in vanilla. Gradually add sugar, blending well. On low speed, alternately mix in milk and dry ingredients. Pour batter into a greased 10-in. cast-iron skillet.
2. Bake at 350° for 25-30 minutes or until the cake springs back when lightly touched. Remove cake and preheat broiler. Combine all topping ingredients and sprinkle over cake. Broil 5 in. from the heat until topping bubbles and turns golden brown. Serve warm.

Nutrition Facts
1 slice: 349 calories, 15g fat (7g saturated fat), 90mg cholesterol, 220mg sodium, 51g carbohydrate (39g sugars, 2g fiber), 5g protein.

Recipe for Lemon-Pepper Tilapia with

Mushrooms

Total Time:Prep/Total time: 25 min   **Makes** :4 servings

Ingredients

- 2 tablespoons butter
- 1/2 pound sliced fresh mushrooms
- 3/4 teaspoon lemon-pepper seasoning, divided
- 3 garlic cloves, minced
- 4 tilapia fillets (6 ounces each)
- 1/4 teaspoon paprika
- 1/8 teaspoon cayenne pepper
- 1 medium tomato, chopped
- 3 green onions, thinly sliced

Directions

1. In a 12-in. skillet, heat butter over medium heat. Add mushrooms and 1/4 teaspoon lemon pepper; cook and stir 3-5 minutes or until tender. Add garlic; cook 30 seconds longer.
2. Place fillets over mushrooms; sprinkle with paprika, cayenne and remaining lemon pepper. Cook, covered, 5-7 minutes or until fish just begins to flake easily with a fork. Top with tomato and green onions.

Nutrition Facts

1 fillet: 216 calories, 8g fat (4g saturated fat), 98mg cholesterol, 173mg sodium, 5g carbohydrate (2g sugars, 1g fiber), 34g protein. Diabetic Exchanges: 4 lean meat, 1-1/2 fat.

Cran-Apple Cobbler

Total Time: **Prep**: 35 min **Bake**: 30 min. **Makes** :8 servings

Ingredients

- 2-1/2 cups sliced peeled apples
- 2-1/2 cups sliced peeled firm pears
- 1 to 1-1/4 cups sugar
- 1 cup fresh or frozen cranberries, thawed
- 1/2 cup water
- 3 tablespoons quick-cooking tapioca
- 3 tablespoons Red Hots
- 1/2 teaspoon ground cinnamon
- 2 tablespoons butter

TOPPING:

3/4 cup all-purpose flour
2 tablespoons sugar
1 teaspoon baking powder
1/4 teaspoon salt
1/4 cup cold butter, cubed
3 tablespoons 2% milk
Vanilla ice cream

Directions

1. In a large cast-iron or other ovenproof skillet, combine the first eight ingredients; let stand for 5 minutes. Cook and stir over medium heat until mixture comes to a full rolling boil, about 18 minutes. Dot with butter.

2. In a small bowl, combine the flour, sugar, baking powder and salt. Cut in butter until mixture resemble coarse crumbs. Stir in milk until a soft dough forms.
3. Drop topping by heaping tablespoons onto hot fruit. Bake at 375° until golden brown, 30-35 minutes. Serve warm with ice cream.

Nutrition Facts

1 serving: 384 calories, 13g fat (8g saturated fat), 38mg cholesterol, 222mg sodium, 67g carbohydrate (48g sugars, 3g fiber), 3g protein.

Gram's Fried Chicken

Total Time: **Prep**: 20 min + chilling   **Cook**: 10 min   **Makes :4 servings**

Ingredients

- 1 large egg
- 1 cup 2% milk
- 2 cups mashed potato flakes
- 1 tablespoon garlic powder
- 1 tablespoon each dried oregano, parsley flakes and minced onion
- 1/2 teaspoon salt
- 1/4 teaspoon coarsely ground pepper
- 4 boneless skinless chicken breast halves (6 ounces each)
- Oil for frying

Directions

1. In a shallow bowl, whisk egg and milk. In another shallow bowl, toss potato flakes with seasonings. Remove half of the potato mixture and reserve (for a second coat of breading).
2. Pound chicken with a meat mallet to 1/2-in. thickness. Dip chicken in egg mixture, then in potato mixture, patting to help coating adhere. Arrange chicken in an even layer on a large plate. Cover and refrigerate chicken and remaining egg mixture 1 hour. Discard remaining used potato mixture.
3. In a 12-in. cast-iron or other deep skillet, heat 1/2 in. of oil over medium heat to 350°. For the second coat of breading, dip chicken in remaining egg mixture, then in unused potato mixture; pat to coat. Fry chicken 4-5 minutes on each side or until golden brown and chicken is no longer pink. Drain on paper towels.

Nutrition Facts

1 chicken breast half : 469 calories, 28g fat (3g saturated fat), 121mg cholesterol, 269mg sodium, 16g carbohydrate (3g sugars, 2g fiber), 38g protein.

Blackened Catfish with Mango Avocado Salsa

Total Time: **Prep**: 20 min + chilling   **Cook**: 10 min**Makes :4 servings(2 cups salsa)**

Ingredients

- 2 teaspoons dried oregano
- 2 teaspoons ground cumin
- 2 teaspoons paprika
- 2-1/4 teaspoons pepper, divided
- 3/4 teaspoon salt, divided
- 4 catfish fillets (6 ounces each)
- 1 medium mango, peeled and cubed
- 1 medium ripe avocado, peeled and cubed
- 1/3 cup finely chopped red onion
- 2 tablespoons minced fresh cilantro

- 2 tablespoons lime juice
- 2 teaspoons olive oil

Directions

1. Combine the oregano, cumin, paprika, 2 teaspoons pepper and 1/2 teaspoon salt; rub over fillets. Refrigerate for at least 30 minutes.
2. Meanwhile, in a small bowl, combine the mango, avocado, red onion, cilantro, lime juice and remaining salt and pepper. Chill until serving.
3. In a large cast-iron skillet, cook fillets in oil over medium heat until fish flakes easily with a fork, 5-7 minutes on each side. Serve with salsa.

Nutrition Facts

1 fillet with 1/2 cup salsa: 376 calories, 22g fat (4g saturated fat), 80mg cholesterol, 541mg sodium, 17g carbohydrate (9g sugars, 6g fiber), 28g protein. Diabetic Exchanges: 5 lean meat, 1 starch, 1/2 fat.

Banana Skillet Upside-Down Cake

Total Time: **Prep**: 25 min **Bake**: 35 min. **Makes** :10 servings

Ingredients

- 1 package (14 ounces) banana quick bread and muffin mix
- 1/2 cup chopped walnuts
- 1/4 cup butter, cubed
- 3/4 cup packed brown sugar
- 2 tablespoons lemon juice
- 4 medium bananas, cut into 1/4-inch slices
- 2 cups sweetened shredded coconut

Directions

1. Preheat oven to 375°. Prepare banana bread batter according to package directions; stir in walnuts.
2. In a 10-in. ovenproof skillet, melt butter over medium heat; stir in brown sugar until dissolved. Add lemon juice; cook and stir until slightly thickened, 2-3 minutes longer. Remove from heat. Arrange bananas in a single layer over brown sugar mixture; sprinkle with coconut.
3. Spoon prepared batter over coconut. Bake until dark golden and a toothpick inserted in center comes out clean, 35-40 minutes. Cool 5 minutes before inverting onto a serving plate. Serve warm.

Nutrition Facts

1 slice: 554 calories, 22g fat (10g saturated fat), 49mg cholesterol, 459mg sodium, 82g carbohydrate (30g sugars, 2g fiber), 6g protein.

One-Skillet Sausage, Peppers, Potatoes, and Onions

PREP TIME: **15 minutes** COOK TIME: **40 minutes** SERVES: **2 to 4**

Ingredients

- 3 tablespoons olive oil, divided
- 4 spicy Italian sausages
- 1 pound baby potatoes, ideally assorted colors, or yellow, halved
- 2 pinches kosher salt, plus more to taste
- 2 bell peppers, roughly chopped (circa 1-inch chunks)
- 1 large red onion, roughly chopped (circa 1-inch chunks)

Directions

1. Set a 10-inch cast-iron skillet over medium-high heat. After it gets good and hot, add the olive oil, then the sausages. Brown all over—about 2 minutes per side—then remove to a waiting plate. We're not trying to cook them through, just sear 'em!
2. Add another tablespoon olive oil to the skillet, followed by the potatoes, cut side facing down. Season with a big pinch of salt. Cook these for 5 minutes until browned, then flip and cook another 5 minutes. Transfer these to the plate with the sausages.
3. Add the remaining tablespoon olive oil, then the peppers and onion. Season with a big pinch of salt. Sauté, stirring occasionally, until tender—about 10 minutes. Add the sausages and potatoes back to the skillet. Pour 1/3 cup water evenly over the top and cover the pan with a lid.
4. Cook for 10 to 15 minutes until the sausage is cooked through and the potatoes are tender, lifting the lid for the last few minutes. Taste and adjust the salt accordingly.

Ina Garten's Skillet-Roasted Lemon Chicken

PREP TIME: 20 minutes **COOK TIME**: 40 minutes **SERVES**: 3

Ingredients
- 2 teaspoons fresh thyme leaves
- 1 teaspoon whole fennel seeds
- Kosher salt and freshly ground black pepper
- 1/3 cup good olive oil
- 1 lemon, halved and sliced 1/4 inch thick (see Notes)
- 1 yellow onion, halved and sliced 1/4 inch thick
- 2 large garlic cloves, thinly sliced
- 1 (4-pound) chicken, backbone removed and butterflied
- 1/2 cup dry white wine, such as Pinot Grigio
- Juice of 1 lemon

Directions
1. Preheat the oven to 450°F.
2. Place the thyme, fennel seeds, 1 tablespoon salt, and 1 teaspoon pepper in a mini food processor and process until ground. Pour the olive oil into a small glass measuring cup, stir in the herb mixture, and set aside.
3. Distribute the lemon slices in a 12-inch cast-iron skillet and distribute the onion and garlic on top. Place the chicken, skin side down, on top of the onion and brush with about half the oil and herb mixture. Turn the chicken skin side up, pat it dry with paper towels (very important!), and brush it all over with the rest of the oil and herb mixture.
4. Roast the chicken for 30 minutes. Pour the wine into the pan (not on the chicken!) and roast for another 10 to 15 minutes, until a meat thermometer inserted into the thickest part of the breast registers 155 to 160°F.
5. Remove the chicken from the oven, sprinkle it with the lemon juice, cover the skillet tightly with aluminum foil, and allow to rest for 10 to 15 minutes. Cut the chicken into quarters or eighths, sprinkle with salt, and serve hot with the pan juices, cooked lemon, and onion.
6. Notes: Remove the ends of the lemon, cut in half through the stem ends, and slice thinly crosswise. Sometimes I sprinkle the chicken with minced fresh rosemary before allowing it to rest.
7. Make Ahead: Assemble the chicken in the pan and refrigerate for a few hours before roasting.

Sunday Steak with French Butter Cast Iron Skillet

Buttermilk Cornbread

Prep: 10 mins **Cook:** 15 mins **Additional:** 5 mins**Total:** 30 mins **Servings:** 8 **Yield:**1 10-inch round
Ingredients

- 1 cup white cornmeal
- ½ cup yellow cornmeal
- ½ cup all-purpose flour
- 4 teaspoons baking powder
- 1 teaspoon salt
- 1 cup buttermilk
- 2 tablespoons lard
- 2 tablespoons vegetable oil
- 1 large egg
- 1 teaspoon butter, or as needed
- 1 pinch paprika
- 1 pinch kosher salt

Directions

1. Place a cast iron skillet in the oven and preheat to 450 degrees F (230 degrees C).
2. Mix white cornmeal, yellow cornmeal, flour, baking powder, and salt together in a large bowl. Add buttermilk, lard, and vegetable oil; stir will to combine. Stir in egg until smooth batter forms.
3. Remove hot cast iron skillet from oven, melt butter in skillet, then pour in batter. Top with paprika and kosher salt. Return skillet to oven.
4. Reduce temperature to 425 degrees F (220 degrees C) and bake until cornbread is golden brown and pulling away from the sides of the pan, about 15 minutes.
5. Remove from oven to cool slightly, about 5 minutes. Cut into wedges.

Cook's Notes:

For a lighter version, you can do the following: substitute the lard and butter with your favorite cooking oil; substitute the buttermilk with 2 percent or skim buttermilk; do not sprinkle mixture top with kosher salt. To turn up the heat: add a 4-ounce can of diced green chiles in the mixture; substitute the paprika with cayenne pepper.

Nutrition Facts
Per Serving:

201.7 calories; protein 4.5g 9% DV; carbohydrates 26.7g 9% DV; fat 8.8g 14% DV; cholesterol 28.9mg 10% DV; sodium 635.1mg 25% DV.

Grandma's Iron Skillet Apple Pie

Prep: 15 mins **Cook:** 45 mins **Additional:** 15 mins**Total:** 1 hr 15 mins **Servings:** 8 **Yield:** 1 apple pie
Ingredients

- ½ cup butter
- 1 cup brown sugar
- 5 eaches Granny Smith apples -- peeled, cored, quartered, and thinly sliced
- 3 (9 inch) refrigerated prerolled pie crusts
- 1 cup white sugar, divided
- 2 teaspoons ground cinnamon, divided
- ¼ cup white sugar
- 1 tablespoon butter, cut into small chunks

Directions

1. Preheat oven to 350 degrees F (175 degrees C).

2. Place 1/2 cup butter into a heavy cast iron skillet, and melt butter in the oven. Remove skillet and sprinkle with brown sugar; return to oven to heat while you prepare the apples.
3. Remove skillet, and place 1 refrigerated pie crust on top of the brown sugar. Top the pie crust with half the sliced apples. Sprinkle apples with 1/2 cup of sugar and 1 teaspoon of cinnamon; place a second pie crust over the apples; top the second crust with the remaining apples, and sprinkle with 1/2 cup sugar and 1 teaspoon cinnamon. Top with the third crust; sprinkle the top crust with 1/4 cup sugar, and dot with 1 tablespoon of butter. Cut 4 slits into the top crust for steam.
4. Bake in the preheated oven until the apples are tender and the crust is golden brown, about 45 minutes. Serve warm.

Nutrition Facts

Per Serving:

734.3 calories; protein 3.4g 7% DV; carbohydrates 107.8g 35% DV; fat 33.7g 52% DV; cholesterol 49.1mg 16% DV; sodium 396.4mg 16% DV.

Spotted Dog Irish Bread

Prep: 15 mins **Cook:** 1 hr **Total:** 1 hr 15 mins **Servings:** 24 **Yield:** 1 12-inch bread

Ingredients

- 5 cups all-purpose flour
- 1 ½ cups white sugar
- 2 ⅔ tablespoons baking powder
- 2 large eggs eggs
- 2 cups milk
- 2 cups raisins

Directions

1. Preheat the oven to 375 degrees F (190 degrees C).
2. Grease a 12-inch cast iron skillet.
3. Sift flour, sugar, and baking powder together in a large bowl.
4. Beat eggs with milk in a separate bowl.
5. Stir egg mixture into flour mixture until moistened; batter will be very thick.
6. Fold in raisins until thoroughly combined.
7. Spread batter into prepared cast iron skillet.
8. Bake in the preheated oven until bread has risen and is golden brown on top, about 1 hour.

Cook's Note:

For two smaller loaves, divide batter into two greased 8-inch round cake pans and bake for 45 minutes.

Nutrition Facts

Per Serving:

196.2 calories; protein 4.3g 9% DV; carbohydrates 43.3g 14% DV; fat 1.1g 2% DV; cholesterol 17.1mg 6% DV; sodium 178.6mg 7% DV.

Hangtown Fry with Parmesan and Fresh Herbs

Prep: 10 mins **Cook:** 15 mins **Total:** 25 mins **Servings:** 3 **Yield:** 3 servings

Ingredients

- 6 large eggs eggs
- ¼ cup heavy cream
- 2 dashes hot pepper sauce
- 1 teaspoon chopped fresh basil
- 1 teaspoon chopped fresh oregano

- ¼ teaspoon freshly ground black pepper
- ⅓ cup freshly grated Parmesan cheese, divided
- 1 teaspoon olive oil
- 1 tablespoon butter
- 12 eaches shucked small oysters, drained
- 2 tablespoons chopped fresh parsley

Directions
1. Preheat the broiler; place the rack about 5 inches from the broiling unit.
2. Whisk eggs in a bowl. Add cream, hot sauce, basil, oregano, black pepper, and 1 tablespoon of the grated Parmesan cheese.
3. Heat oil in a skillet over medium-high heat. Melt the butter in the skillet and swirl it around to coat the pan evenly. Place the oysters in the skillet and brown on both sides, about 1 minute on each side. Let the liquid reduce a bit, about 30 seconds longer.
4. Slowly pour the egg mixture over the oysters, keeping the oysters evenly distributed in the pan. After about 30 seconds, shake the pan slightly but do not stir. After about 3 minutes when the bottom and sides of the eggs begin to set, sprinkle the remaining cheese on top and place the pan under the broiler.
5. Broil until the eggs begin to puff around the edges and the top is nicely browned, 5 to 7 minutes. Remove from the oven; sprinkle with chopped parsley. Serve immediately from the skillet in wedge-shaped pieces.

Nutrition Facts
Per Serving:

558.7 calories; protein 44.1g 88% DV; carbohydrates 17.4g 6% DV; fat 33.5g 52% DV; cholesterol 513.8mg 171% DV; sodium 675.1mg 27% DV.

Cast Iron Buttermilk Biscuits

Prep: 25 mins **Cook:** 20 mins**Total:** 45 mins **Servings:** 24**Yield:** 2 dozen

Ingredients
- 1 ⅓ cups buttermilk
- 2 large eggs eggs
- 4 cups all-purpose flour
- 5 teaspoons baking powder
- 1 teaspoon cream of tartar
- 1 teaspoon salt

Directions
1. Preheat oven to 425 degrees F (220 degrees C). Place 1 tablespoon butter in two 10-inch cast iron skillets.
2. Place skillets in the preheated oven to heat up and melt butter, 5 to 10 minutes.
3. Mix buttermilk and eggs together in a small bowl.
4. Combine flour, baking powder, cream of tartar, and salt in a large bowl. Rub in remaining 6 tablespoons butter with your fingers until mixture is crumbly. Gently stir in buttermilk mixture until dough just starts to come together.
5. Turn dough out onto a lightly floured work surface. Pat into a rectangle about 1/2 inch thick. Cut dough into 24 biscuits.
6. Remove skillets from the oven. Arrange 12 biscuits side-by-side in each, their edges touching.
7. Return skillets to the oven and bake until biscuits are puffed and lightly browned, 15 to 20 minutes.

Cook's Note:

If you like the bottoms softer, allow the skillets to cool briefly before adding biscuits in .

Nutrition Facts
Per Serving:
122 calories; protein 3.2g 6% DV; carbohydrates 16.9g 6% DV; fat 4.6g 7% DV; cholesterol 26.2mg 9% DV; sodium 246.3mg 10% DV.

Pork Tenderloin alla Napoli

Prep: 15 mins **Cook:** 40 mins**Total:** 55 mins **Servings:** 6 **Yield:** 6 servings

Ingredients

- 1 tablespoon olive oil
- 2 (3/4 pound) pork tenderloins
- 2 plum tomato (blank)s Roma (plum) tomatoes, seeded and chopped
- ¼ cup chopped green olives
- ¼ cup dry white wine
- 1 teaspoon chopped fresh rosemary
- 2 cloves garlic, minced
- ½ teaspoon salt
- ¼ teaspoon pepper
- ½ cup heavy cream

Directions

1. Preheat oven to 400 degrees F (200 degrees C). Heat the oil in a cast iron skillet over medium-high hea Brown pork on all sides in the skillet.
2. Mix the tomatoes, olives, wine, rosemary and garlic in a bowl. Pour over the pork. Season with salt an pepper.
3. Place skillet with pork in the preheated oven, and bake 30 minutes, to a minimum internal temperature of 145 degrees F (63 degrees C).
4. Remove pork from skillet, leaving remaining tomato mixture and juices. Place skillet over medium hea and gradually mix in the cream. Stirring constantly, bring to a boil. Reduce heat to low, and continue cooking 5 minutes, until thickened. Slice pork, and drizzle with the cream sauce to serve.

Nutrition Facts
Per Serving:
206.7 calories; protein 18g 36% DV; carbohydrates 2.1g 1% DV; fat 13g 20% DV; cholesterol 75.6mg 25 DV; sodium 381mg 15% DV.

Corn Tortillas

Prep: 20 mins **Cook:** 15 mins **Additional:** 30 mins**Total:** 1 hr 5 mins **Servings:** 5 **Yield:** 15 tortillas

Ingredients

- 1 ¾ cups masa harina
- 1 ⅛ cups water

Directions

1. In a medium bowl, mix together masa harina and hot water until thoroughly combined. Turn dough o a clean surface and knead until pliable and smooth. If dough is too sticky, add more masa harina; if it begins to dry out, sprinkle with water. Cover dough tightly with plastic wrap and allow to stand for 30 minutes.
2. Preheat a cast iron skillet or griddle to medium-high.

3. Divide dough into 15 equal-size balls. Using a tortilla press, a rolling pin, or your hands, press each ball of dough flat between two sheets of plastic wrap.
4. Immediately place tortilla in preheated pan and allow to cook for approximately 30 seconds, or until browned and slightly puffy. Turn tortilla over to brown on second side for approximately 30 seconds more, then transfer to a plate. Repeat process with each ball of dough. Keep tortillas covered with a towel to stay warm and moist until
5. ready to serve.

Nutrition Facts
Per Serving:

145.6 calories; protein 3.7g 8% DV; carbohydrates 30.4g 10% DV; fat 1.5g 2% DV; cholesterolmg; sodium 3.6mg.

Cast-Iron Skillet Prime Rib Roast and Gravy

Prep: 15 mins **Cook:** 3 hrs **Additional:** 15 mins**Total:** 3 hrs 30 mins **Servings:**8 **Yield:** 1 beef roast

Ingredients

- 1 (4.5 pound) beef prime rib roast at room temperature
- 2 teaspoons coarse sea salt, or as needed
- 2 teaspoons freshly ground black pepper, or as needed
- 1 onion, quartered
- ¼ cup unsalted butter
- ¼ cup all-purpose flour
- ¼ cup red wine
- 1 (32 ounce) carton beef stock
- 4 sprigs fresh thyme

Directions

1. Preheat oven to 275 degrees F (135 degrees C).
2. Rub beef roast with sea salt and black pepper. Heat a large cast-iron skillet over medium-high heat; sear roast on all sides in the hot skillet, 2 to 3 minutes per side. Turn roast so the ribs and fat side are facing up.
3. Roast prime rib in the preheated oven for 45 minutes; scatter onion quarters around roast and continue cooking until an instant-read meat thermometer inserted into the thickest part of the meat reads 130 degrees F (54 degrees C) for rare, about 2 more hours.
4. Remove roast from skillet, wrap meat in aluminum foil, and let rest for 15 to 20 minutes to let juices reabsorb into the meat. Leave onion pieces in skillet.
5. Pour drippings from skillet into a bowl and skim off excess grease. Return degreased drippings to skillet with onion pieces, place over medium heat, and melt butter in the drippings. Whisk flour into mixture to make a paste, 1 to 2 minutes. Stir red wine into flour paste until smooth. Mix beef stock into pan gravy until smooth; stir thyme sprigs into gravy.
6. Reduce heat to low and simmer gravy until thickened, 5 to 8 minutes. Strain gravy, discard onion pieces and thyme, and serve with prime rib.

Nutrition Facts
Per Serving:

562.2 calories; protein 27.6g 55% DV; carbohydrates 7.9g 3% DV; fat 45.2g 70% DV; cholesterol 110.1mg 37% DV; sodium 557.5mg 22% DV.

Sausage Biscuits and Gravy

Prep: 10 mins **Cook:** 20 mins**Total:** 30 mins **Servings:** 4 **Yield:** 4 servings

Ingredients

- 1 (19 ounce) can Southern-style flaky refrigerated biscuits (such as Pillsbury Grands)
- 1 (16 ounce) package maple-flavored breakfast sausage
- 3 tablespoons all-purpose flour, or as needed
- 1 (12 ounce) can evaporated milk
- 1 ½ cups milk
- ½ teaspoon salt
- ¼ teaspoon ground black pepper
- 1 teaspoon butter

Directions

1. Preheat oven to 350 degrees F (175 degrees C).
2. Arrange biscuits about 1 1/2 inches apart on a baking sheet.
3. Bake in the preheated oven until golden brown, 13 to 17 minutes. Slice cooked biscuits in half crosswi: and keep warm.
4. While biscuits are baking, crumble sausage into a large skillet over medium heat; cook, breaking meat apart, until no longer pink inside, about 10 minutes. Sprinkle sausage and pan drippings with flour and cook and stir until sausage is coated, about 1 more minute. Reduce heat to medium-low.
5. Pour evaporated milk into sausage mixture, followed by milk; stir until thoroughly combined. Bring to simmer, stirring constantly, and cook until gravy is your desired thickness, 3 to 5 minutes. Season with salt and ground black pepper. Stir butter into gravy until melted. Stir in more flour if gravy isn't thick enough.
6. Place biscuits with cut sides up on serving plates; top with sausage gravy.

Nutrition Facts
Per Serving:
947 calories; protein 38.4g 77% DV; carbohydrates 66.1g 21% DV; fat 59.8g 92% DV; cholesterol 128.5r 43% DV; sodium 3110.9mg 124% DV.

Old Fashioned Pineapple Upside-Down Cake

Prep: 25 mins **Cook:** 30 mins **Additional:** 5 mins **Total:** 1 hr **Servings:** 12 **Yield:** 1 10-inch round cake

Ingredients

- 4 large eggs eggs
- ½ cup butter
- 1 cup packed light brown sugar
- 1 (20 ounce) can sliced pineapple
- 10 cherries maraschino cherries, halved
- 1 cup sifted cake flour
- 1 teaspoon baking powder
- ¼ teaspoon salt
- 1 cup white sugar
- 1 tablespoon butter, melted
- 1 teaspoon almond extract

Directions

1. Preheat oven to 325 degrees F (165 degrees C).
2. In a 10-inch heavy skillet with a heat-resistant handle (I use a cast iron skillet), melt 1/2 cup butter ov very low heat. Remove from heat, and sprinkle brown sugar evenly over pan. Arrange pineapple slice to cover bottom of skillet. Distribute cherries around pineapple; set aside.

3. Sift together flour, baking powder, and salt.
4. Separate the eggs into two bowls. In a large bowl, beat egg whites just until soft peaks form. Add granulated sugar gradually, beating well after each addition. Beat until medium-stiff peaks form. In a small bowl, beat egg yolks at high speed until very thick and yellow. With a wire whisk or rubber scraper, using an over-and-under motion, gently fold egg yolks and flour mixture into whites until blended. Fold in 1 tablespoon melted butter or margarine and almond extract. Spread batter evenly over pineapple in skillet.
5. Bake until surface springs back when gently pressed with fingertip and a toothpick inserted in the center comes out clean, about 30 to 35 minutes. Loosen the edges of the cake with table knife. Cool the cake for 5 minutes before inverting onto serving plate.

Nutrition Facts
Per Serving:
321.1 calories; protein 3.2g 6% DV; carbohydrates 55g 18% DV; fat 10.4g 16% DV; cholesterol 84.9mg 28% DV; sodium 183.1mg 7% DV.

Cajun Blackened Catfish

Prep: 10 mins **Cook:** 10 mins **Total:** 20 mins **Servings:** 4 **Yield:** 4 servings

Ingredients

* 1 teaspoon ground black pepper
* 1 teaspoon garlic powder
* 1 teaspoon onion powder
* 1 teaspoon paprika
* 1 teaspoon dried parsley
* 1 teaspoon ground cayenne pepper
* 1 teaspoon kosher salt
* ½ teaspoon dried oregano
* ½ teaspoon dried thyme
* 4 (4 ounce) catfish fillets, skinned
* ¾ cup unsalted butter

Directions

1. In a shallow bowl, mix together the black pepper, garlic powder, onion powder, paprika, parsley, cayenne pepper, kosher salt, oregano, and thyme until thoroughly combined. Press the catfish fillets into the spice mixture to thoroughly coat.
2. Arrange a portable heat source outdoors, such as a butane burner or side burner of a gas grill. Melt butter in a glass or metal bowl. Light the burner, and place a large cast-iron skillet onto the burner over high heat. Pour about 1/4 cup of melted butter into the skillet; set remaining 1/2 cup of butter aside.
3. When the butter in the skillet is smoking hot, lay the catfish fillets into the skillet. Cook until the spices are burned onto the fillets and the catfish is opaque and flaky inside, about 3 minutes per side. Don't breathe smoke from burning spices. To serve, pour remaining 1/2 cup of butter over the catfish.

Cook's Note
This recipe is for cooking OUTSIDE only because of the intense smoking.

Nutrition Facts
Per Serving:
466.3 calories; protein 18.2g 36% DV; carbohydrates 2.2g 1% DV; fat 43.2g 67% DV; cholesterol 144.1mg 48% DV; sodium 545.7mg 22% DV.

Aebleskiver

Prep: 15 mins Cook: 15 minsTotal: 30 mins Servings: 30 Yield: 30 aebleskivers

Ingredients

- 2 large egg whites egg whites
- 2 cups all-purpose flour
- 2 teaspoons baking powder
- 1 tablespoon white sugar
- ½ teaspoon baking soda
- ½ teaspoon salt
- 2 large egg yolks egg yolks
- 4 tablespoons butter, melted
- 2 cups buttermilk
- 1 cup vegetable oil for frying

Directions

1. In a clean glass or metal bowl, beat the egg whites with an electric mixer until they can hold a stiff pea Set aside.
2. Mix together the flour, baking powder, salt, baking soda, sugar, egg yolks, melted butter and buttermil at one time and beat until smooth. Gently fold in the egg whites last.
3. Put about 1tablespoon of vegetable oil in the bottom of each aebleskiver pan cup and heat until hot. Pc in about 2 tablespoons of the batter into each cup. As soon as they get bubbly around the edge, turn the quickly (Danish cooks use a long knitting needle, but a fork will work). Continue cooking, turning the ball to keep it from burning.

Nutrition Facts

Per Serving:

63.3 calories; protein 1.8g 4% DV; carbohydrates 7.7g 3% DV; fat 2.8g 4% DV; cholesterol 18.4mg 6% DV; sodium 124.7mg 5% DV.

Skillet Strawberry Pancake

Prep: 5 mins Cook: 25 minsTotal: 30 mins Servings: 4 Yield: 1 8-inch pancake

Ingredients

- 3 large eggs large eggs
- ¾ cup whole milk
- ½ teaspoon vanilla extract
- ¼ cup white sugar
- ¼ teaspoon salt
- ½ cup all-purpose flour
- 2 tablespoons unsalted butter
- 1 cup sliced fresh strawberries

Directions

1. Preheat an oven to 425 degrees F (220 degrees C).
2. Place the eggs, milk, vanilla extract, sugar, salt, and flour into a blender. Pulse until no dry lumps rem in the batter. Melt the butter in an 8-inch, cast iron skillet over medium-high heat. Pour in the batter, a drop in the strawberries.
3. Place the skillet into the oven, and bake until puffed and golden, 20 to 25 minutes. Remove from the oven and serve immediately.

Variations

1. Cinnamon: add 1/2 teaspoon of cinnamon to the batter. Skip strawberries.
2. Apple: slice 1/2 an apple and cook it on the melted butter until lightly golden. You may add a pinch o

cinnamon to it. Skip strawberries.

3. Blueberry: use 1/2 cup of blueberries instead of strawberries.
4. Banana: add 1 sliced banana to the melted butter and cook it until golden, but still firm. You may add a pinch of cinnamon to it. Skip strawberries.
5. Chocolate chip: add 1/2 cup of your favorite chocolate chip to the batter in the skillet. Skip strawberries.
6. Chocolate: add 1 tablespoon of cocoa to the batter.
7. Plain: skip strawberries and top baked pancake with a squeeze of lemon juice and powdered sugar.

Nutrition Facts
Per Serving:

252.1 calories; protein 8.1g 16% DV; carbohydrates 30g 10% DV; fat 11.3g 17% DV; cholesterol 159.3mg 53% DV; sodium 217.7mg 9% DV.

Deep-Dish Cast Iron Pizza

Prep: 20 mins **Cook:** 40 mins **Additional:** 1 hr 15 mins**Total:** 2 hrs 15 mins **Servings:** 6 **Yield:** 1 12-inch pizza

Ingredients

- 2 ¼ teaspoons active dry yeast
- ½ teaspoon brown sugar
- 1 ¼ cups warm water (110 degrees F (43 degrees C))
- 2 cups all-purpose flour
- 2 teaspoons garlic salt
- ¼ cup butter
- 2 cups all-purpose flour
- 1 tablespoon grapeseed oil
- 1 serving cooking spray
- ⅓ cup bulk pork sausage
- 1 (3.5 ounce) link bulk Italian sausage
- 2 tablespoons grapeseed oil
- ½ cup pizza sauce
- ⅓ cup shredded mozzarella cheese
- 24 slices pepperoni
- ⅓ cup shredded mozzarella cheese
- 1 tablespoon butter, softened
- ⅛ teaspoon Italian seasoning
- ⅛ teaspoon garlic powder

Directions

1. Sprinkle yeast and brown sugar over warm water in the bowl of a stand mixer fitted with a dough hook. Let stand 5 to 10 minutes until the yeast softens and begins to form a creamy foam.
2. Turn mixer to the lowest setting and slowly add 2 cups flour 1/2 cup at a time. Add garlic salt and 1/4 cup butter. Integrate remaining 2 cups flour and knead until dough is smooth and elastic, 5 to 7 minutes.
3. Coat a large glass bowl with 1 tablespoon grapeseed oil. Shape dough into a ball and place in bowl, turning to coat all sides with oil. Spray a piece of plastic wrap with cooking spray and loosely cover bowl. Cover bowl with a towel and let rise in a warm area until dough has doubled in size, about 45 minutes. Punch down dough and allow to rest for 20 minutes.
4. While dough is resting, heat a skillet over medium heat; cook and stir bulk sausage until browned and crumbly, about 5 minutes. Transfer cooked sausage to a bowl with a slotted spoon, retaining drippings in the skillet. Fry Italian sausage link in drippings until browned and no longer pink in the center, about 10

minutes. Slice sausage.

5. Preheat oven to 400 degrees F (200 degrees C). Grease a 12-inch cast iron skillet with 2 tablespoons grapeseed oil.

6. Press dough into and up the sides of the prepared skillet. Poke holes in dough with a fork to prevent a bubbles. Spread pizza sauce around the base of the crust. Sprinkle 1/3 cup mozzarella cheese over sau layer half the bulk sausage, half the sliced sausage, and half the pepperoni over cheese. Repeat the lay of meat. Top with remaining 1/3 cup mozzarella cheese.

7. Bake in preheated oven on the bottom rack until crust is golden brown, about 25 minutes. Brush crust with 1 tablespoon butter; season with Italian seasoning and garlic powder. Remove pizza from skillet and let rest for 3 to 5 minutes before slicing.

Cook's Note:

This pairs perfectly with a caesar salad! My cast iron skillet is 12-inches - if your cast iron skillet is small you will have excess dough. Please do NOT try making this in a regular skillet. Please note this is meant a cast iron skillet and I can't promise similar results if you attempt making this in a regular skillet.

Nutrition Facts

Per Serving:

615.9 calories; protein 17.4g 35% DV; carbohydrates 67.2g 22% DV; fat 30.2g 46% DV; cholesterol 57.7mg 19% DV; sodium 1148.6mg 46% DV.

Irish Soda Bread in a Skillet

Prep: 10 mins **Cook:** 15 mins**Total:** 25 mins **Servings:** 8 **Yield:** 8 servings

Ingredients

- 1 cup milk
- 1 teaspoon vinegar
- 2 cups all-purpose flour
- ½ teaspoon salt
- ½ teaspoon baking soda

Directions

1. Preheat the oven to 400 degrees F (200 degrees C). In a cup or small bowl, stir together the milk and vinegar. Let stand 10 minutes, or until curdled.

2. In a medium bowl, stir together the flour, salt and baking soda. Stir in the curdled milk mixture until smooth. Scrape the dough out of the bowl onto a floured surface, and shape into a disc. Place the disc into a cast iron skillet.

3. Bake for 15 minutes in the preheated oven, or until the crust feels firm to the touch.

Nutrition Facts

Per Serving:

129 calories; protein 4.2g 9% DV; carbohydrates 25.3g 8% DV; fat 0.9g 1% DV; cholesterol 2.4mg 1% DV; sodium 237.1mg 10% DV.

Prep: 20 mins **Cook:** 20 mins**Total:** 40 mins **Servings:** 4 **Yield:** 4 servings

Ingredients

- ½ pound sage pork sausage (such as Jimmy Dean)
- 1 ½ cups cubed red potatoes
- ½ onion, diced
- 1 tablespoon chopped garlic
- 1 cup sliced baby bella mushrooms

- 3 large eggs eggs
- 1 teaspoon parsley
- ½ cup shredded Mexican cheese blend
- 1 pinch sea salt to taste
- 1 pinch fresh cracked black pepper to taste

Directions

1. Place sausage in a large cast iron skillet over medium heat; cook and stir until crumbly and starting to brown, about 5 minutes. Stir in potatoes; cook until starting to brown, about 5 minutes. Add onion and garlic; cook and stir until fragrant, about 3 minutes. Stir in mushrooms; cook until tender, about 5 minutes.
2. Push mixture to the sides of the skillet with a spatula to make space in the center. Crack eggs into the center and sprinkle with parsley. Sprinkle Mexican cheese blend around mixture on the edges. Cover skillet and cook until egg whites are set but yolk is still runny, 2 to 3 minutes. Remove from heat, pierce yolks and mix to combine. Season with salt and black pepper.

Cook's Note:

You may need to add a little olive oil to cook the eggs in .

Nutrition Facts
Per Serving:

302.7 calories; protein 17.4g 35% DV; carbohydrates 13.5g 4% DV; fat 20g 31% DV; cholesterol 184.4mg 62% DV; sodium 728.5mg 29% DV.

DJ's Outdoor Pork Loin with Veggies

Prep: 40 mins **Cook:** 1 hr **Additional:** 1 day**Total:** 1 day **Servings:** 8 **Yield:** 8 servings

Ingredients

- 2 tablespoons packed dark brown sugar
- 2 teaspoons sea salt
- 1 tablespoon paprika
- 1 teaspoon ground cumin
- ½ teaspoon black pepper
- 1 teaspoon cayenne pepper
- 1 tablespoon garlic powder
- 1 tablespoon rubbed sage
- 1 (2 pound) pork loin
- ½ cup olive oil
- 4 eaches red potatoes, quartered
- 2 eaches sweet potatoes, quartered
- 5 medium (blank)s carrots, cut into 1-inch chunks
- 1 large onion, quartered
- 2 tablespoons sea salt
- 1 teaspoon ground black pepper
- 1 tablespoon chopped fresh cilantro
- 3 large apples, cored and sliced
- 3 cups fresh orange juice
- ½ cup lemon juice

Directions

1. Mix the brown sugar, 2 teaspoons sea salt, paprika, cumin, 1/2 teaspoon black pepper, cayenne pepper, garlic powder, and sage in a small bowl. Pat the pork loin completely dry with paper towels. Rub the mixture onto the pork loin to coat completely.
2. Pour the olive oil into a large resealable plastic bag. Add the seasoned loin to the bag and seal. Allow to marinate in the refrigerator for 24 hours, turning the bag once to assure an even flavor.
3. Place the red potatoes, sweet potatoes, carrots, and onion in a large pot and cover with water. Add the 2 tablespoon salt, 1 teaspoon pepper, and cilantro to the water. Bring to a boil, reduce heat to low and allow to continue on a slow boil for 25 minutes; drain, reserving the water.
4. Preheat an outdoor grill for high heat and lightly oil grate.
5. Remove the pork loin from the bag. Sear on the preheated grill, 4 to 5 minutes per side; remove and set aside. Reduce grill heat to medium.
6. Place a 12-inch cast-iron skillet on the grill. Lay the apple slices on the bottom of the skillet. Pour the orange juice and lemon juice into the skillet. Place the pork loin on the apples. Arrange the drained vegetables around the pork loin. Pour reserved water into the skillet to fill within 1/2 inch of top.
7. Cook on grill for 1 hour, pouring more of reserved water over the pork after 30 minutes.

Nutrition Facts

Per Serving:

493.2 calories; protein 21.7g 43% DV; carbohydrates 49.9g 16% DV; fat 24.1g 37% DV; cholesterol 55.2mg 18% DV; sodium 1871.5mg 75% DV.

Campfire S'mores Smash

Prep: 5 mins **Cook:** 20 mins **Additional:** 2 hrs**Total:** 2 hrs 25 mins **Servings:** 10 **Yield:** 10 servings

Ingredients

- 1 tablespoon butter
- 1 (10 ounce) package mini marshmallows
- 2 individual packages graham crackers, crumbled
- 2 (1.5 ounce) bars chocolate candy bars, broken into pieces

Directions

1. Melt the butter in a cast iron pan over the slow, red embers of your campfire. Pour in marshmallows, and stir until completely melted. Remove from the fire, and stir in the graham crackers and chocolate. Press into the pan with the back of a spoon. Allow to cool completely, then cut into wedges.

Nutrition Facts

Per Serving:

283 calories; protein 2.5g 5% DV; carbohydrates 51.6g 17% DV; fat 6.8g 11% DV; cholesterol 5.1mg 2% DV; sodium 229.4mg 9% DV.

Moist Vegan Cornbread

Prep: 10 mins **Cook:** 25 mins**Additional:** 5 mins**Total:** 40 mins **Servings:** 12 **Yield:** 1 10-inch skillet

Ingredients

- 2 cups soy milk
- 2 teaspoons apple cider vinegar
- 2 cups cornmeal
- 1 cup all-purpose flour
- 2 teaspoons baking powder
- ½ teaspoon salt
- ⅓ cup canola oil
- 2 tablespoons maple syrup
- 1 cup frozen corn kernels

Directions

1. Preheat oven to 350 degrees F (175 degrees C). Place a greased, 10-inch cast iron skillet in the preheating oven.
2. Mix soy milk and vinegar together in a bowl. Let stand until curdled, about 5 minutes.
3. Mix cornmeal, flour, baking powder, and salt together in a bowl.
4. Pour oil and maple syrup into the soy milk mixture. Whisk with a fork until foamy, about 3 minutes. Pour over cornmeal mixture and mix until combined. Fold in corn kernels. Pour batter into the hot skillet.
5. Bake in the preheated oven until a toothpick inserted into the center comes out clean, 25 to 35 minutes. Slice into squares or wedges.

Cook's Note:

You can also use honey instead of maple syrup, but then the cornbread is no longer vegan.

Nutrition Facts

Per Serving:

209.7 calories; protein 4.5g 9% DV; carbohydrates 31.4g 10% DV; fat 7.9g 12% DV; cholesterolmg; sodium 206.9mg 8% DV.

Bacon Sweet Potato Cornbread

Prep: 15 mins **Cook:** 40 mins**Total:** 55 mins**Servings:** 6 **Yield:** 1 9-inch skillet

Ingredients

- 5 slices bacon
- 1 ¼ cups cornmeal
- 1 teaspoon salt
- ½ teaspoon baking soda
- 1 cup mashed cooked sweet potato
- 1 cup buttermilk
- 2 large eggs eggs, lightly beaten

Directions

1. Preheat oven to 450 degrees F (230 degrees C).
2. Cook and stir bacon in a 9-inch cast-iron skillet over medium-high heat until browned, about 10 minutes. Remove and chop bacon, leaving 1 tablespoon of bacon drippings in skillet.
3. Whisk cornmeal, salt, and baking soda in a bowl. Stir sweet potato, buttermilk, and eggs together in a separate bowl until thoroughly combined. Stir sweet potato mixture into dry ingredients and mix chopped bacon into batter. Pour batter into the cast-iron skillet.
4. Bake corn bread in the preheated oven until browned and bread feels firm to the touch, about 30 minutes. Turn corn bread onto a serving plate and cut into wedges for serving.

Nutrition Facts

Per Serving:

206.8 calories; protein 8.7g 17% DV; carbohydrates 29.4g 10% DV; fat 5.7g 9% DV; cholesterol 72.1mg 24% DV; sodium 750mg 30% DV.

Danish Ebelskiver

Prep: 20 mins **Cook:** 10 mins**Total:** 30 mins **Servings:** 7 **Yield:** 7 pancakes

Ingredients

- 3 large eggs eggs, separated
- 2 cups half-and-half cream

- 2 teaspoons white sugar
- ½ teaspoon salt
- 2 cups all-purpose flour
- 1 teaspoon baking powder
- 1 teaspoon baking soda
- 1 teaspoon ground cinnamon
- 1 tablespoon melted butter, or as needed

Directions
1. Beat the egg yolks in a bowl; whisk the half-and-half, sugar, and salt with the egg yolks until thoroughly mixed.
2. Whisk the flour, baking powder, baking soda, and cinnamon together in a separate bowl. Beat the flour mixture into the egg mixture just until smooth and most of the lumps are gone.
3. With an electric mixer, beat the egg whites in a bowl until they form stiff peaks. Gently fold the beaten egg whites into the batter.
4. Brush melted butter into the round depressions of a cast-iron ebelskiver pan. Place the pan over medium-high heat. When the butter is very hot and smells slightly nutty, pour batter into each depression, filling the round shapes about half to three-quarters full. Allow the ebelskiver to cook until the bottoms are golden brown, 1 to 2 minutes. The inside batter will still be runny.
5. Using a toothpick or wooden skewer, gently push each ebelskiver at an edge to loosen from the pan. Insert the toothpick lightly into a top edge from the inside, and gently lift and rotate the pancake to turn it over. Turn them so the round bottoms are facing upward and the liquid batter in the center of a pancake runs into the bottom of the round depression. Cook until the other side of each pancake is browned, about 1 more minute.
6. Remove the finished pancakes from the pan with the toothpick, transfer to a platter, and serve warm.

Nutrition Facts
Per Serving:
270.8 calories; protein 8.5g 17% DV; carbohydrates 32g 10% DV; fat 12.1g 19% DV; cholesterol 109.7mg 37% DV; sodium 486.3mg 20% DV.

Cary's Cast Iron Skillet Chicken Recipe
 Prep: 15 mins **Cook:** 46 mins **Additional:** 5 mins**Total:** 1 hr 6 mins **Servings:** 4 **Yield:** 4 chicken breasts
Ingredients
- 2 tablespoons olive oil
- 1 onion, chopped
- ½ bell pepper, chopped
- 6 medium (blank)s mushrooms, sliced, or more to taste
- 2 cloves garlic, minced, or more to taste
- 1 tablespoon oregano, or more to taste
- 1 tablespoon basil, or more to taste
- 1 teaspoon paprika, or more to taste
- 1 teaspoon ground black pepper, or more to taste
- 1 pinch salt to taste
- 1 (16 ounce) can black beans, rinsed and drained
- 1 cup uncooked rice
- 4 breast half, bone and skin removed (blank)s skinless, boneless chicken breast halves
- 1 (28 ounce) can crushed tomatoes
- 2 cups water, divided, or as needed

Directions

1. Preheat oven to 350 degrees F (175 degrees C).
2. Heat oil in a cast iron skillet over medium heat; stir in onion. Cook and stir until the onion is softened and lightly browned, about 8 minutes. Lower heat and add bell pepper, mushrooms, and garlic; cook and stir until soft, 3 to 5 minutes more.
3. Mix oregano, basil, paprika, black pepper, and salt together in a bowl. Stir 1/2 of the herb mixture into vegetable mixture. Stir black beans and rice into vegetable mixture. Arrange chicken breasts over beans and rice mixture, sprinkle remaining herb mixture on top. Pour in tomatoes and 1 cup water. Cover skillet with aluminum foil.
4. Bake until chicken is no longer pink in the center and the juices run clear, adding more water as needed to keep mixture moist, about 25 minutes. Remove aluminum foil and cook until rice is soft, adding more water as needed to keep mixture moist, 10 to 15 minutes more. Remove skillet from oven and set aside to cool slightly, 5 to 10 minutes.

Cook's Notes:

If you don't have a cast iron skillet, you can transfer mixture to a baking dish before placing in the oven. This recipe will work for up to 6 chicken breasts, if desired.

Nutrition Facts

Per Serving:

537.9 calories; protein 38.3g 77% DV; carbohydrates 72.7g 24% DV; fat 10.9g 17% DV; cholesterol 67.2mg 22% DV; sodium 825mg 33% DV.

Grandma's Leftover Turkey Pot Pie

Prep: 20 mins **Cook:** 55 mins **Additional:** 30 mins**Total:** 1 hr 45 mins **Servings:** 8 **Yield:** 1 10-inch deep dish pie

Ingredients

- 2 ½ cups all-purpose flour
- ½ teaspoon salt
- 1 cup chilled solid vegetable shortening
- 6 tablespoons ice water, or as needed
- 3 cups cubed cooked turkey
- ½ small onion, chopped
- 1 (10.75 ounce) can cream of potato soup
- 1 (10.75 ounce) can cream of chicken soup
- ½ (10.75 ounce) can water
- 2 (15 ounce) cans mixed vegetables, drained
- 1 pinch salt and pepper to taste

Directions

1. Whisk together the flour and 1/2 teaspoon of salt in a bowl. Cut the shortening into the flour mixture with a pastry cutter until the mixture looks like coarse crumbs. Drizzle the ice water, about 1 tablespoon at a time, over the mixture and gently work the water into the dough with your fingers. Add more water as needed until you can gather the dough together in a ball. Wrap the dough in plastic wrap and refrigerate for 30 minutes.
2. Preheat oven to 375 degrees F (190 degrees C).
3. In a saucepan, mix together the turkey, onion, cream of potato soup, cream of chicken soup, water, and mixed vegetables. Bring the mixture to a boil; reduce heat and allow to simmer while you prepare the crust.
4. Cut the dough in almost equal halves. Roll the larger piece into a circle on a floured work surface and fit

into a 10-inch cast-iron skillet. Roll out the smaller piece into a circle to fit the top. Pour the hot turkey filling into the bottom crust. Place top crust over the filling, crimp the two crusts together with a fork, and cut several slits in the top with a sharp knife.

5. Bake in the preheated oven until the crust is golden brown, about 45 minutes.

Nutrition Facts

Per Serving:

559.3 calories; protein 22.5g 45% DV; carbohydrates 45g 15% DV; fat 31.7g 49% DV; cholesterol 44.5mg 15% DV; sodium 911.5mg 37% DV.

Bubba's Beer Bread

Prep: 15 mins **Cook:** 1 hr**Total:** 1 hr 15 mins **Servings:** 8 **Yield:** 8 servings

Ingredients

- 3 cups self-rising flour
- 3 tablespoons white sugar
- 1 teaspoon onion powder
- 1 teaspoon dried dill, or to taste
- 1 teaspoon salt
- 1 (12 fluid ounce) can beer, room temperature
- 4 ounces cubed Cheddar cheese, or to taste

Directions

1. Preheat the oven to 350 degrees F (175 degrees C). Lightly grease a 9 or 10 inch cast iron skillet.
2. In a large bowl, stir together the self-rising flour, sugar, onion powder, dill weed and salt. Pour in the beer, and stir until all of the dry is incorporated. Stir as lightly as possible so as not to deflate the beer. Fold in cheese cubes.
3. Bake for 45 to 60 minutes, or until the top springs back when lightly touched. The bread should rise w. above the edge of the pan.

Nutrition Facts

Per Serving:

261.6 calories; protein 8.4g 17% DV; carbohydrates 41.5g 13% DV; fat 5.2g 8% DV; cholesterol 14.9mg 5% DV; sodium 976.2mg 39% DV.

Cheesy Pizza Rolls

Total Time: **Prep:** 15 min **Bake:** 25 min.**Makes** :8 appetizers

Ingredients

- 1 loaf (1 pound) frozen pizza dough, thawed
- 1/2 cup pasta sauce
- 1 cup shredded part-skim mozzarella cheese, divided
- 1 cup coarsely chopped pepperoni (about 64 slices)
- 1/2 pound bulk Italian sausage, cooked and crumbled
- 1/4 cup grated Parmesan cheese
- Minced fresh basil, optional
- Crushed red pepper flakes, optional

Directions

1. Preheat oven to 400°. On a lightly floured surface, roll dough into a 16x10-in. rectangle. Brush with pasta sauce to within 1/2 in. of edges.
2. Sprinkle with 1/2 cup mozzarella cheese, pepperoni, sausage and Parmesan. Roll up jelly-roll style, starting with a long side; pinch seam to seal. Cut into 8 slices. Place in a greased 9-in. cast-iron skillet

greased 9-in. round baking pan, cut side down.
3. Bake 20 minutes; sprinkle with remaining mozzarella cheese. Bake until golden brown, 5-10 minutes longer. If desired, serve with minced fresh basil and crushed red pepper flakes.

Test Kitchen tips
1. If you have a favorite homemade or store-bought fresh dough, swap it for the frozen dough.
2. Give rolls a little room in the pan to stretch their wings. They will expand in the oven.
3. Prefer a crisper pizza crust? Bake an additional 5 to 10 minutes.

Nutrition Facts
1 appetizer: 355 calories, 19g fat (7g saturated fat), 42mg cholesterol, 978mg sodium, 29g carbohydrate (3g sugars, 0 fiber), 14g protein.

Skillet Herb Bread

Total Time: **Prep**: 10 min **Bake**: 35 min.**Makes** :10 servings

Ingredients
- 1-1/2 cups all-purpose flour
- 2 tablespoons sugar
- 4 teaspoons baking powder
- 1-1/2 teaspoons salt
- 1 teaspoon rubbed sage
- 1 teaspoon dried thyme
- 1-1/2 cups yellow cornmeal
- 1-1/2 cups chopped celery
- 1 cup chopped onion
- 1 jar (2 ounces) chopped pimientos, drained
- 3 large eggs, room temperature, beaten
- 1-1/2 cups fat-free milk
- 1/3 cup vegetable oil

Directions
1. In a large bowl, combine the flour, sugar, baking powder, salt, sage and thyme. Combine cornmeal, celery, onion and pimientos; add to dry ingredients and mix well. Add eggs, milk and oil; stir just until moistened. Pour into a greased 10- or 11-in. ovenproof skillet. Bake at 400° for 35-45 minutes or until bread tests done. Serve warm.

Nutrition Facts
1 slice: 275 calories, 9g fat (2g saturated fat), 57mg cholesterol, 598mg sodium, 40g carbohydrate (6g sugars, 2g fiber), 7g protein.

Baked Cheddar Eggs & Potatoes

Total Time:**Prep/Total time**: 30 min **Makes** :4 servings

Ingredients
- 3 tablespoons butter
- 1-1/2 pounds red potatoes, chopped
- 1/4 cup minced fresh parsley
- 2 garlic cloves, minced
- 3/4 teaspoon kosher salt
- 1/8 teaspoon pepper
- 8 large eggs
- 1/2 cup shredded extra-sharp cheddar cheese

Directions

1. Preheat oven to 400°. In a 10-in. cast-iron or other ovenproof skillet, heat butter over medium-high hea
   Add potatoes; cook and stir until golden brown and tender. Stir in parsley, garlic, salt and pepper. With
   the back of a spoon, make 4 wells in the potato mixture; break 2 eggs into each well.
2. Bake until egg whites are completely set and yolks begin to thicken but are not hard, 9-11 minutes.
   Sprinkle with cheese; bake until cheese is melted, 1 minute.

Nutrition Facts

1 serving: 395 calories, 23g fat (12g saturated fat), 461mg cholesterol, 651mg sodium, 29g carbohydrate (3
sugars, 3g fiber), 19g protein.

Italian Sausage Veggie Skillet

Total Time:Prep/Total time: 30 min**Makes** :6 servings

Ingredients

- 4 cups uncooked whole wheat spiral pasta
- 1 pound Italian turkey sausage, casings removed
- 1 medium onion, chopped
- 1 garlic clove, minced
- 2 medium zucchini, chopped
- 1 large sweet red pepper, chopped
- 1 large sweet yellow pepper, chopped
- 1 can (28 ounces) diced tomatoes, drained
- 1/4 teaspoon salt
- 1/4 teaspoon pepper

Directions

1. Cook pasta according to package directions; drain.
2. Meanwhile, in large skillet, cook sausage and onion over medium-high heat until sausage is no longer
   pink, 5-7 minutes. Add garlic and cook 1 minute longer. Add zucchini and peppers; cook until crisp-
   tender, 3-5 minutes. Add tomatoes, salt and pepper. Cook and stir until vegetables are tender and begin
   to release their juices, 5-7 minutes. Serve with pasta.

Nutrition Facts

1-1/3 cups: 251 calories, 6g fat (1g saturated fat), 28mg cholesterol, 417mg sodium, 35g carbohydrate (4g
sugars, 6g fiber), 16g protein. Diabetic exchanges: 2 vegetable, 2 lean meat, 1-1/2 starch.

Sweet Potato and Egg Skillet

Total Time:Prep/Total time: 25 min**Makes** :4 servings

Ingredients

- 2 tablespoons butter
- 2 medium sweet potatoes, peeled and shredded (about 4 cups)
- 1 garlic clove, minced
- 1/2 teaspoon salt, divided
- 1/8 teaspoon dried thyme
- 2 cups fresh baby spinach
- 4 large eggs
- 1/8 teaspoon coarsely ground pepper

Directions

1. In a large cast-iron or other heavy skillet, heat the butter over low heat. Add sweet potatoes, garlic, 1/4 teaspoon salt and thyme; cook, covered, until potatoes are almost tender, 4-5 minutes, stirring occasionally. Stir in spinach just until wilted, 2-3 minutes.
2. With the back of a spoon, make 4 wells in potato mixture. Break an egg into each well. Sprinkle eggs with pepper and remaining salt. Cook, covered, on medium-low until egg whites are completely set and yolks begin to thicken but are not hard, 5-7 minutes.

Test Kitchen tips
1. If you like your eggs sunny-side up, leave the pan uncovered while they cook.
2. Break the eggs into a small dish before adding to the pan. It's easier to remove stray shell pieces if they get into the egg.
3. Health tip: With the sweet potatoes and spinach, this dish meets the daily requirement for vitamin A

Nutrition Facts

1 serving: 224 calories, 11g fat (5g saturated fat), 201mg cholesterol, 433mg sodium, 24g carbohydrate (10g sugars, 3g fiber), 8g protein. Diabetic Exchanges: 1-1/2 starch, 1-1/2 fat, 1 medium-fat meat.

Spicy Veggie Pasta Bake

Total Time:Prep/Total time: 30 min**Makes :**6servings

Ingredients
* 3 cups uncooked spiral pasta
* 1 medium yellow summer squash
* 1 small zucchini
* 1 medium sweet red pepper
* 1 medium green pepper
* 1 tablespoon olive oil
* 1 small red onion, halved and sliced
* 1 cup sliced fresh mushrooms
* 1/2 teaspoon salt
* 1/4 teaspoon pepper
* 1/4 teaspoon crushed red pepper flakes
* 1 jar (24 ounces) spicy marinara sauce
* 8 ounces fresh mozzarella cheese pearls
* Grated Parmesan cheese and julienned fresh basil, optional

Directions
1. Preheat oven to 375°. Cook pasta according to package directions for al dente; drain.
2. Cut squashes and peppers into 1/4-in. julienne strips. In a 12-in. cast-iron or other ovenproof skillet, heat oil over medium-high heat. Add onion, mushrooms and julienned vegetables; cook and stir until crisp-tender, 5-7 minutes. Stir in seasonings. Add marinara sauce and pasta; toss to combine. Top with cheese pearls.
3. Transfer to oven; bake, uncovered, until cheese is melted, 10-15 minutes. If desired, sprinkle with Parmesan cheese and basil before serving.

Nutrition Facts

1-1/3 cups (calculated without grated Parmesan cheese): 420 calories, 13g fat (6g saturated fat), 32mg cholesterol, 734mg sodium, 57g carbohydrate (12g sugars, 5g fiber), 17g protein.

Flavorful Chicken Fajitas

Total Time: **Prep**: 20 min + marinating **Cook**: 10 min. **Makes :**6 servings

Ingredients
* 4 tablespoons canola oil, divided

- 2 tablespoons lemon juice
- 1-1/2 teaspoons seasoned salt
- 1-1/2 teaspoons dried oregano
- 1-1/2 teaspoons ground cumin
- 1 teaspoon garlic powder
- 1/2 teaspoon chili powder
- 1/2 teaspoon paprika
- 1/2 teaspoon crushed red pepper flakes, optional
- 1-1/2 pounds boneless skinless chicken breast, cut into thin strips
- 1/2 medium sweet red pepper, julienned
- 1/2 medium green pepper, julienned
- 4 green onions, thinly sliced
- 1/2 cup chopped onion
- 6 flour tortillas (8 inches), warmed
- Optional: Shredded cheddar cheese, taco sauce, salsa, guacamole, sliced red onions and sour cream

Directions
1. In a large bowl, combine 2 tablespoons oil, lemon juice and seasonings; add the chicken. Turn to coat; cover. Refrigerate for 1-4 hours.
2. In a large cast-iron or other heavy skillet, saute peppers and onions in remaining oil until crisp-tender. Remove and keep warm.
3. Drain chicken, discarding marinade. In the same skillet, cook chicken over medium-high heat until no longer pink, 5-6 minutes. Return pepper mixture to pan; heat through.
4. Spoon filling down the center of tortillas; fold in half. Serve with desired toppings.

Nutrition Facts

1 fajita: 369 calories, 15g fat (2g saturated fat), 63mg cholesterol, 689mg sodium, 30g carbohydrate (2g sugars, 1g fiber), 28g protein. Diabetic Exchanges: 3 lean meat, 2 starch, 2 fat.

Cinnamon-Sugar Apple Pie **Mary's Cast Iron Skillet Cornbread**

Prep: 10 mins **Cook:** 30 mins **Total:** 40 mins **Servings:** 8 **Yield:** 1 10-inch round

Ingredients
- 1 tablespoon vegetable oil
- 1 (14 ounce) can cream-style corn
- 1 ½ cups self-rising yellow cornmeal
- ½ cup buttermilk
- ½ cup sour cream
- ½ cup Greek yogurt
- 2 large eggs eggs, beaten
- ½ teaspoon salt
- ¼ teaspoon ground red chile pepper, or to taste
- 1 tablespoon butter, or to taste

Directions
1. Pour vegetable oil in a cast iron skillet; place in the oven. Preheat oven to 400 degrees F (200 degrees C).

2. Mix cream-style corn, cornmeal, buttermilk, sour cream, yogurt, eggs, salt, and red chile pepper together in a bowl to form batter. Remove skillet from oven using oven mitts; pour in batter.
3. Bake in the preheated oven until edges pull away from skillet, 30 to 40 minutes. Spread butter over top.

Cook's Note:

Buttermilk can be substituted with milk, if desired.

Nutrition Facts

Per Serving:

210.9 calories; protein 6.1g 12% DV; carbohydrates 27g 9% DV; fat 9.8g 15% DV; cholesterol 60.1mg 20% DV; sodium 631.5mg 25% DV.

Finally, A Perfect Fried Chicken Recipe

Prep: 20 mins **Cook:** 50 mins **Additional:** 3 hrs **Total:** 4 hrs 10 mins **Servings:** 6 **Yield:** 6 servings

Ingredients

- 6 medium (blank)s chicken leg quarters, cut into thighs and drumsticks
- 3 cups buttermilk
- 1 cup all-purpose flour
- 2 teaspoons onion powder
- 2 teaspoons garlic powder
- 2 teaspoons seasoned salt
- 1 ½ teaspoons chicken bouillon granules
- ¾ teaspoon crumbled dried sage
- ½ teaspoon ground black pepper
- ¼ teaspoon ground thyme
- 1 pinch dried marjoram
- 2 large eggs eggs
- ½ cup milk
- 1 cup vegetable oil for frying, or as needed

Directions

1. Place chicken thighs and drumsticks into a bowl and pour buttermilk over chicken. Stir to coat. Cover and marinate in refrigerator for 3 hours (or up to overnight).
2. Preheat oven to 425 degrees F (220 degrees C).
3. Place flour, onion powder, garlic powder, seasoned salt, chicken bouillon granules, sage, black pepper, thyme, and marjoram into a 1-gallon resealable plastic bag. Close bag and shake to combine flour and seasonings. Whisk eggs and milk in a large bowl.
4. Pour vegetable oil into a cast-iron skillet or an oven-safe glass or metal pan. Heat skillet with oil in the hot oven for 10 minutes.
5. While oil is heating, drain buttermilk from chicken pieces and place each chicken piece into plastic bag of seasoned flour. Seal bag and shake to coat chicken piece with seasoned flour. Dip each coated piece in egg mixture, then return the piece to the bag of flour mixture and shake to coat a second time. Place coated chicken pieces onto a plate to rest for 5 minutes to set coating.
6. Place coated chicken into hot oil in the skillet and bake for 30 minutes. Turn chicken over and bake until no longer pink inside and the coating is golden brown, about 20 more minutes. Place chicken pieces on a rack to drain oil before serving.

Cook's Notes:

You can substitute 3 cups water plus 1 tablespoon salt for buttermilk if desired. Bake boneless chicken breasts for a total of 30 minutes (15 minutes on each side).

Nutrition Facts

Per Serving:

491.3 calories; protein 50.5g 101% DV; carbohydrates 24.8g 8% DV; fat 20g 31% DV; cholesterol 211.5m 71% DV; sodium 698.7mg 28% DV.

Cast Iron Corn Bread

Prep: 15 mins **Cook:** 27 mins **Total:** 42 mins **Servings:** 8 **Yield:** 1 10-inch round

Ingredients

- 2 large eggs eggs
- 1 ½ cups milk
- 2 ½ cups self-rising white cornmeal
- ½ teaspoon salt
- 3 tablespoons vegetable oil
- 2 tablespoons shortening

Directions

1. Preheat oven to 450 degrees F (230 degrees C).
2. Whisk eggs together in a large bowl until light and frothy; stir in milk. Stir in cornmeal and salt. Add o stir until batter is smooth.
3. Place shortening in a 10-inch cast iron skillet; heat skillet in the preheated oven until shortening is liquefied, 2 to 3 minutes. Remove skillet and pour in batter.
4. Return skillet to oven and bake until corn bread is lightly browned, 25 to 30 minutes.
5. Remove skillet from oven immediately and cover with wooden cutting board. Use oven mitts to invert skillet and tip corn bread onto cutting board. Cut into 8 wedges.

Cook's Notes:

If you're not using self-rising cornmeal, add about 1 teaspoon baking powder to your recipe.
For true Southern taste, fry up some bacon in your skillet beforehand and use it instead of the shortening.
Do not leave corn bread in skillet after baking, or you will have a crumbly, broken mess on your hands.

Nutrition Facts

Per Serving:

242 calories; protein 6.2g 13% DV; carbohydrates 29g 9% DV; fat 11.8g 18% DV; cholesterol 50.2mg 17 DV; sodium 657mg 26% DV.

Basil and Prosciutto-Wrapped Halibut

Prep: 5 mins **Cook:** 11 mins **Total:** 16 mins **Servings:** 2 **Yield:** 2 servings

Ingredients

- 6 leaves basil
- 2 slices prosciutto
- 2 (4 ounce) fillets halibut
- ½ teaspoon adobo seasoning
- 1 tablespoon olive oil

Directions

1. Preheat oven to 400 degrees F (200 degrees C).
2. Lay 3 basil leaves on each slice of prosciutto. Season the halibut fillets with Adobo seasoning, place them on one side of the prepared slices of prosciutto, and wrap the fish fillets with the prosciutto and basil.
3. Set an oven-safe skillet over medium-high heat. When the skillet is hot, pour in the olive oil and place the wrapped halibut fillets in the pan.
4. Cook the fillets until the prosciutto is golden brown, about 4 minutes. Flip the fillets over and move th

pan into the preheated oven. Bake until the fish is firm to the touch
5.   and cooked through, about 5 minutes.

Nutrition Facts
Per Serving:
239.7 calories; protein 26.5g 53% DV; carbohydrates 0.3g; fat 14g 22% DV; cholesterol 49mg 16% DV; sodium 340.1mg 14% DV.

White Bean, Turkey, and Sausage Chili

Prep: 20 mins **Cook:** 50 mins**Total:** 1 hr 10 mins **Servings:** 6 **Yield:** 6 servings

Ingredients

- 1 (1 ounce) package hot Italian sausage links
- 1 tablespoon olive oil
- 2 eaches turkey cutlets, cut into bite sized pieces
- 1 tablespoon ground cumin
- 1 ½ teaspoons garlic powder
- 1 pinch salt and ground black pepper to taste
- 2 eaches onions, chopped
- 8 cloves garlic
- 4 (15 ounce) cans white kidney beans (cannellini), rinsed and drained
- 3 (10.75 ounce) cans low-sodium chicken broth
- 1 tablespoon ground cumin
- 1 ½ teaspoons garlic powder
- 2 peppers jalapeno peppers, chopped
- 2 peppers whole jalapeno peppers

Directions

1.   Preheat oven to 350 degrees F (175 degrees C).
2.   Wrap the sausages in foil, place them on a baking sheet, and bake for 30 minutes.
3.   Heat olive oil in a large cast-iron pan over medium-high heat. Cook and stir turkey in hot oil until evenly browned, about 5 minutes.
4.   Season turkey with 1 tablespoon cumin, 1 1/2 teaspoons garlic powder, salt, and black pepper. Add onions and garlic to the turkey; continue to cook and stir until onion is softened, 5 to 7 minutes.
5.   Pour in the white kidney beans and chicken broth. Season with 1 tablespoon cumin and 1 1/2 teaspoons garlic powder. Simmer over medium heat, stirring occasionally, for 30 minutes.
6.   Mix in the chopped jalapeno and the whole jalapeno peppers, if desired. Remove the sausages from the oven and cut them into bite-sized pieces. Stir the sausage into the chili.
7.   Cook the chili until the whole jalapeno peppers are tender and chili is thick, about 15 minutes more.

Cook's Note:
You can use Hot Italian Turkey Sausage instead of pork, if you prefer. Whole jalapenos are optional, but tasty!

Nutrition Facts
Per Serving:
588.4 calories; protein 40.9g 82% DV; carbohydrates 52.3g 17% DV; fat 22.9g 35% DV; cholesterol 73.1mg 24% DV; sodium 1322.3mg 53% DV.

PREP TIME: 6 hours 10 minutes **COOK TIME**: 16 minutes **MAKES**: 4 servings

Ingredients

- 2 porterhouse steaks, 1 pound each
- 1 pinch Kosher salt
- 1 stick unsalted butter
- 1 1/2 tablespoons flat leaf parsley, chopped
- 1/2 teaspoon garlic, minced
- 1 teaspoon shallot, minced
- 1 pinch Freshly ground white pepper
- 1/2 fresh lemon
- 1 splash Oil

Directions

1. At least 6 hours before and up to the day before you plan to cook the steaks place them on a cooling ra set over a tray with edges. You want to catch the drips.
2. Season both sides of the steaks with salt. Put them back into the fridge uncovered until an hour before you want to cook them.
3. Allow the butter to soften at room temperature. Meanwhile place the garlic, shallot and parsley into a mortar. Using the pestle bruise, crush, and pulverize the aromatics until they are mushy.
4. Place the butter into a small mixing bowl and smear it around with a rubber spatula. Add the aromatics a few drops of lemon juice, a pinch of salt and a few grinds of white pepper. Blend the butter until it is one shade of green with no streaks.
5. You can either refrigerate the butter as is or you can roll it up in parchment pepper, then foil and twist the ends to form a round log. The foil allows the ends to stay sealed.
6. When your are ready to cook the steaks, season both sides with fresh ground black pepper. Place a cas iron skillet over medium high heat. Add enough oil to coat the bottom of the pan. When the oil is hot - you don't want it too hot but you want it to start searing right away -- add the steak. Cook the steak on both sides until it is very brown and caramelized. Remove the steak from the pan when it has reached one temperature below where you like. If you want it cooked medium then cook the steak to medium rare and so on. Remove the steak to a sheet tray.
7. Cook the second steak in the same fashion. Both steaks can be cooked up to an hour in advance and le to sit at room temperature. Do not refrigerate them.
8. In your oven place the top rack so it is about 8 to 10 inches from the broiler. Heat the broiler.
9. Using a filet knife cut the meat from each side of the bone then slice the meat into smaller bit size pieces. Re-assemble the steaks on the sheet tray. Smear each steak with some softened maitre d'butter then place a small glob on each steak.
10. Place the steaks under the broiler just long enough to melt the butter and heat the steaks through. Serv

The Best Pan-Roasted Potatoes Vegan Double Chocolate-Peanut Butter Skillet Cookie

Prep: 15 minsCook: 35 mins **Additional:** 15 minsTotal: 1 hr 5 mins **Servings:** 12 **Yield:** 1 10-inch skill cookie

Ingredients

- 1 cup all-purpose flour
- ½ cup unsweetened cocoa powder
- 1 teaspoon baking soda
- ¼ teaspoon salt
- 2 tablespoons water
- 1 tablespoon dry egg replacer (such as Bob's Red Mill)

- ½ cup vegan butter, softened
- ½ cup white sugar
- ½ cup packed light brown sugar
- 1 teaspoon vanilla extract
- 1 (10 ounce) package vegan chocolate mini chips (such as Enjoy Life)
- ¼ cup creamy peanut butter

Directions
1. Preheat the oven to 350 degrees F (175 degrees C).
2. Whisk flour, cocoa, baking soda, and salt together in a medium bowl.
3. Combine water and egg replacer in a small bowl. Mix well and let sit until thickened, about 1 minute.
4. Cream vegan butter, white sugar, and brown sugar together in the bowl of a stand mixer until light and fluffy, about 3 minutes. Mix in egg replacer and vanilla. Gradually mix in dry ingredients until combined. Fold in chocolate chips.
5. Transfer 1/2 of the dough into a well seasoned 10-inch cast iron skillet. Press down with your fingers to distribute evenly over the bottom of the skillet. Spread peanut butter over the dough. Press remaining dough on top of the peanut butter; it's okay if some peanut butter is poking through.
6. Bake in the preheated oven until top is firm to the touch and dry and edges have started to pull away from the sides of the skillet, 35 to 40 minutes.
7. Remove from the oven and let cool for 15 to 20 minutes before slicing; cookie will firm up as it cools.

Nutrition Facts
Per Serving:
326.1 calories; protein 4.7g 9% DV; carbohydrates 41.6g 13% DV; fat 20.2g 31% DV; cholesterolmg; sodium 256.7mg 10% DV.

Country Sausage Gravy

Prep: 15 mins **Cook:**20 mins**Total:** 35 mins **Servings:** 4 **Yield:** 4 servings

Ingredients
- 1 pound pork sausage
- 1 onion, finely chopped
- 1 green bell pepper, finely chopped
- 1 teaspoon crushed red pepper flakes
- 2 tablespoons garlic, minced
- 4 tablespoons unsalted butter
- salt and pepper to taste
- 4 tablespoons all-purpose flour
- 1 teaspoon minced fresh sage
- 1 teaspoon minced fresh thyme
- 2 cups milk, divided
- 2 cubes chicken bouillon
- ¼ cup minced fresh parsley

Directions
1. In a skillet on medium heat cook pork, onion, green pepper, red pepper flakes, and garlic until pork is crumbly. Drain off excess fat, but leave a small amount.
2. Combine butter, salt, and pepper with the meat mixture and stir until butter melts. Slowly sift flour over the top. Mix gently and allow mixture to cook for 5 minutes. It will burn, so do not let it sit unguarded. Don't forget to scrape the bottom of the pan. Add the sage and thyme.

3. Slowly stir in milk, about a half a cup at a time, and incorporate it well. When the mixture thickens, add more milk. Do not let it boil vigorously, or it will burn. Add chicken bullion and let cook for five minutes. Again, if it thickens too much, add more milk. Adjust taste with more salt and pepper if needed.
4. Just before serving, add the parsley, and about a 1/4 cup more milk; the gravy will thicken quickly as it cools.

Nutrition Facts
Per Serving:
700.1 calories; protein 19.7g 39% DV; carbohydrates 20.3g 7% DV; fat 60.1g 93% DV; cholesterol 117.8mg 39% DV; sodium 1389.3mg 56% DV.

Almond Skillet Cake

Prep:5 mins **Cook:** 40 mins **Additional:** 50 mins**Total:** 1 hr 35 mins **Servings:** 9 **Yield:** 9 servings

Ingredients
- 1 serving cooking spray
- 1 ½ cups all-purpose flour
- 1 ½ cups white sugar
- 1 ½ sticks unsalted butter, melted
- 1 large egg
- 1 teaspoon almond flavoring
- 1 pinch sea salt

Topping:
- ¼ cup sliced almonds
- 2 tablespoons white sugar

Directions
1. Preheat the oven to 350 degrees F (175 degrees C). Line a 10-inch cast iron skillet with aluminum foil with the ends hanging over. Spray lightly with cooking spray.
2. Combine flour, sugar, butter, egg, almond flavoring, and salt in a bowl. Mix well. Pour batter into the prepared cast iron pan and smooth it level. Sprinkle top with almonds and sugar.
3. Bake in the preheated oven until lightly browned, about 40 minutes.
4. Cool cake in the pan for 20 minutes. Carefully lift the cake out of the pan and cool completely on a rack about 30 minutes more. Top cooled cake with a second rack and flip over. Carefully remove foil and f onto a serving plate. Cut and serve.

Nutrition Facts
Per Serving:
376.4 calories; protein 3.6g 7% DV; carbohydrates 52.5g 17% DV; fat 17.5g 27% DV; cholesterol 61.3m 20% DV; sodium 45.8mg 2% DV.

English Toffee

Prep: 5 mins **Cook:** 15 mins**Total:** 20 mins **Servings:** 16 **Yield:**16 servings

Ingredients
- 1 cup butter
- 1 ¼ cups white sugar
- 2 tablespoons water
- ¼ cup slivered almonds
- 1 cup chocolate chips

Directions

1. Butter a 10x15 inch jellyroll pan.
2. Melt butter in a heavy skillet over medium heat. Stir in sugar and water. Bring to a boil and add almonds. Cook, stirring constantly until nuts are toasted and the sugar is golden. Pour the mixture into the prepared pan; do not spread.
3. Immediately sprinkle the chocolate chips on top. Let stand for a minute, then spread the chocolate over the top. Let cool completely, then break into pieces.

Nutrition Facts
Per Serving:

222.2 calories; protein 0.9g 2% DV; carbohydrates 22.6g 7% DV; fat 15.5g 24% DV; cholesterol 30.5mg 10% DV; sodium 82.9mg 3% DV.

Black and Blue Steak Burger

Prep: 20 mins **Cook:** 25 mins **Additional:** 30 mins**Total:** 1 hr 15 mins **Servings:** 4 **Yield:** 4 burgers

Ingredients

- ¾ pound fatty rib-eye steak
- ¾ pound top sirloin steak
- 2 ounces blue cheese
- 1 pinch salt and freshly ground black pepper to taste
- 1 ½ tablespoons mayonnaise, or to taste
- 4 eaches hamburger buns, split and toasted
- 2 ounces pickled red onions, or to taste

Direction

1. Slice steaks in half, then into strips about 1/4-to 1/2-inch-thick. Place in a bowl and cover with plastic wrap. Freeze until very cold and firm, but not quite frozen, about 30 minutes to 1 hour. Place blue cheese in the freezer as well so it's easier to handle.
2. Chop the partially frozen steak with a sharp knife or meat cleaver until it resembles coarsely ground meat. Crumble about 1/2 cup (unpacked) blue cheese on top; use the cleaver to fold and chop it into the meat.
3. Lightly dampen your hands with water and roll the mixture into 3 or 4 patties. Flatten onto individual pieces of plastic wrap; seal and refrigerate until ready to cook.
4. Unwrap patties and continue pressing them to your desired thinness. Season both sides with salt and pepper.
5. Heat a dry cast iron pan over medium-high heat until very hot. Sear each patty, without disturbing it, until a crust forms on the bottom, about 3 minutes. Flip and continue cooking until the surface springs back when lightly pressed, about 3 minutes more.
6. Spread some mayonnaise over each bottom bun half. Serve patties on the buns, topped with pickled red onions.

Chef's Notes:

This will also work with cheaper cuts like chuck, or round, but there's a certain luxury to starting out with meat that's already tender before it's even chopped. If you can find some extra flavorful dry-aged beef, this will be even more memorable.

Feel free to use no cheese, or a different variety, but the blue cheese promises impressive crustification.

To make your own quick-pickled red onions, season 1 sliced red onion with a big pinch of salt, cover with red wine vinegar, and refrigerate overnight, or until the onions turn color and soften slightly.

Nutrition Facts
Per Serving:

435.5 calories; protein 30.9g 62% DV; carbohydrates 23.9g 8% DV; fat 23.1g 36% DV; cholesterol 79.6mg

27% DV; sodium 915.4mg 37% DV.

Skillet Hasselback Sweet Potatoes

Total Time: **Prep**: 25 min **Bake**: 45 min.**Makes :8 servings**

Ingredients

- 8 small sweet potatoes (about 7 ounces each)
- 1/2 cup butter, melted
- 3 tablespoons finely chopped shallot
- 3 garlic cloves, minced
- 1-1/2 teaspoons salt
- 1/2 teaspoon fresh ground pepper
- 2 teaspoons minced fresh parsley
- 2 teaspoons minced fresh thyme
- 2 teaspoons minced fresh sage
- 1/2 cup soft whole wheat bread crumbs
- 1/4 cup grated Parmesan cheese
- 1/2 cup chopped toasted nuts, optional

Directions

1. Preheat oven to 425°. Cut thin slices lengthwise from bottom of sweet potatoes to allow them to lie fla discard slices. Place potatoes flat side down; cut crosswise into 1/8-in. slices, leaving them intact at the bottom. Arrange sweet potatoes in a 12-in. cast-iron or other ovenproof skillet.
2. Stir together next 5 ingredients. Spoon half the butter mixture evenly over sweet potatoes. Bake 35 minutes.
3. Meanwhile, add herbs to remaining butter mixture. Toss bread crumbs with Parmesan. Remove skillet from oven. Spoon remaining butter mixture over potatoes; top with bread crumb mixture. Return to ov until potatoes are tender and topping is golden brown, 10-12 minutes. If desired, top with toasted nuts.

Nutrition Facts

1 sweet potato: 333 calories, 13g fat (8g saturated fat), 33mg cholesterol, 620mg sodium, 52g carbohydra (20g sugars, 6g fiber), 5g protein.

Rolled Buttermilk Biscuits

Total Time: **Prep**: 20 min **Bake**: 15 min.**Makes :8 servings**

Ingredients

- 2 cups all-purpose flour
- 3 teaspoons baking powder
- 1/2 teaspoon baking soda
- 1/4 teaspoon salt
- 3 tablespoons cold butter
- 3/4 to 1 cup buttermilk
- 1 tablespoon fat-free milk

Directions

1. Preheat oven to 450°. In a large bowl, combine the flour, baking powder, baking soda and salt; cut in butter until mixture resembles coarse crumbs. Stir in enough buttermilk just to moisten dough.
2. Turn onto a lightly floured surface; knead 3-4 times. Pat or roll to 3/4-in. thickness. Cut with a floured 1/2-in. biscuit cutter. Place in a large ungreased cast-iron or other ovenproof skillet.
3. Brush with milk. Bake until golden brown, 12-15 minutes.

Nutrition Facts

1 biscuit: 162 calories, 5g fat (3g saturated fat), 12mg cholesterol, 412mg sodium, 25g carbohydrate (1g sugars, 1g fiber), 4g protein. Diabetic Exchanges: 1-1/2 starch, 1 fat.

One-Skillet Pasta

Total Time: **Prep**: 20 min **Bake**: 1-1/4 hours.**Makes :5 servings**

Ingredients

- 1-1/2 pounds ground turkey
- 1 medium onion, finely chopped
- 1 medium sweet red pepper, finely chopped
- 1 can (28 ounces) diced tomatoes, undrained
- 1 can (14-1/2 ounces) fire-roasted diced tomatoes, undrained
- 1 can (14-1/2 ounces) reduced-sodium beef broth
- 1 can (4 ounces) sliced mushrooms, drained
- 1 tablespoon packed brown sugar
- 1 tablespoon chili powder
- 8 ounces uncooked angel hair pasta
- 1 cup shredded cheddar cheese

Directions

1. In a large cast-iron or other heavy skillet, cook the turkey, onion and pepper over medium heat until meat is no longer pink; drain.
2. Add the tomatoes, broth, mushrooms, brown sugar and chili powder. Bring to a boil. Reduce heat; simmer, uncovered, for 30 minutes.
3. Add pasta; return to a boil. Reduce heat; cover and simmer until pasta is tender, 30-35 minutes. Sprinkle with cheese. Cover and cook until cheese is melted, 2-3 minutes longer.

Nutrition Facts

Nutrition Facts: 1-2/3 cups equals 621 calories, 28 g fat (11 g saturated fat), 118 mg cholesterol, 967 mg sodium, 58 g carbohydrate, 7 g fiber, 36 g protein.

Deluxe Cornbread Stuffing

Total Time: **Prep**: 20 min **Bake**: 55 min.**Makes :12 servings**

Ingredients

- 6 cups crumbled cornbread
- 2 cups white bread cubes, toasted
- 1 cup chopped pecans
- 1/4 cup minced fresh parsley
- 1 teaspoon dried thyme
- 1/2 teaspoon rubbed sage
- 1/2 teaspoon salt
- 1/2 teaspoon pepper
- 1 pound bulk pork sausage
- 2 tablespoons butter
- 2 large tart apples, diced
- 1 cup diced celery
- 1 medium onion, finely chopped
- 1-3/4 to 2-1/4 cups chicken broth

Directions

1. In a large bowl, combine the bread, pecans and seasonings; set aside. Crumble sausage into a large cast iron or other ovenproof skillet; cook over medium heat until no longer pink, breaking into crumbles. Remove with slotted spoon; drain on paper towels.
2. Add butter to drippings; saute the apples, celery and onion until tender. Add to bread mixture; stir in sausage and enough broth to moisten.
3. Spoon mixture into cast-iron skillet; cover and bake at 350° for 45 minutes. Uncover and bake just until set, about 10 minutes.

Nutrition Facts

1 cup: 326 calories, 18g fat (4g saturated fat), 19mg cholesterol, 780mg sodium, 35g carbohydrate (8g sugars, 4g fiber), 8g protein.

Muenster Bread

Total Time: **Prep**: 20 min + rising   **Bake**: 55 min.+ cooling**Makes :1 loaf (16 slices)**

Ingredients

- 2 packages (1/4 ounce each) active dry yeast
- 1 cup warm 2% milk (110° to 115°)
- 1/2 cup butter, softened
- 2 tablespoons sugar
- 1 teaspoon salt
- 3-1/4 to 3-3/4 cups all-purpose flour
- 1 large egg plus 1 large egg yolk, room temperature
- 4 cups shredded Muenster cheese
- 1 large egg white, beaten

Directions

1. In a large bowl, dissolve yeast in milk. Add the butter, sugar, salt and 2 cups flour; beat until smooth. Stir in enough remaining flour to form a soft dough.
2. Turn onto a floured surface; knead until smooth and elastic, 6-8 minutes. Place in a greased bowl, turning once to grease top. Cover and let rise in a warm place until doubled, about 1 hour.
3. In a large bowl, beat egg and yolk; stir in cheese. Punch down dough; roll into a 16-in. circle.
4. Place in a greased 10-in. cast-iron skillet or 9-in. round baking pan, letting dough drape over the edges. Spoon the cheese mixture into center of dough. Gather dough up over filling in 1-1/2-in. pleats. Gently squeeze pleats together at top and twist to make a topknot. Let rise 10-15 minutes.
5. Brush loaf with egg white. Bake at 375° for 40-45 minutes. Cool on a wire rack for 20 minutes. Serve warm.

Nutrition Facts

1 slice: 273 calories, 16g fat (9g saturated fat), 71mg cholesterol, 399mg sodium, 22g carbohydrate (3g sugars, 1g fiber), 11g protein.

Rhubarb Crisp

Total Time: **Prep**: 15 min **Bake**: 45 min**Makes :8 servings**

Ingredients

- 3/4 cup sugar
- 3 tablespoons cornstarch
- 3 cups sliced fresh rhubarb or frozen rhubarb, thawed
- 2 cups sliced peeled apples or sliced

strawberries

- 1 cup quick-cooking or old-fashioned oats
- 1/2 cup packed brown sugar
- 1/2 cup butter, melted
- 1/3 cup all-purpose flour
- 1 teaspoon ground cinnamon
- Vanilla ice cream, optional

Directions

1. In a large bowl, combine sugar and cornstarch. Add rhubarb and apples or strawberries; toss to coat. Spoon into an 8-in. cast-iron skillet or other ovenproof skillet.
2. In a small bowl, combine the oats, brown sugar, butter, flour and cinnamon until the mixture resembles coarse crumbs. Sprinkle over fruit. Bake at 350° until crisp is bubbly and fruit is tender, about 45 minutes. If desired, serve warm with ice cream.

Test Kitchen Tips

1. Cinnamon comes in two basic types: Ceylon and cassia. Ceylon cinnamon's delicate, complex flavor is ideal for ice creams and simple sauces. The spicy, bolder cassia cinnamon (often labeled simply as cinnamon) is preferred for baking.
2. Dark brown sugar contains more molasses than light or golden brown sugar. The types are generally interchangeable in recipes. But if you prefer a bolder flavor, choose dark brown sugar.
3. Get inspired by these delicious easy desserts.

Nutrition Facts

1 cup: 320 calories, 12g fat (7g saturated fat), 31mg cholesterol, 124mg sodium, 52g carbohydrate (36g sugars, 3g fiber), 3g protein.

Gnocchi Chicken Skillet

Total Time:Prep/Total time: 20 min**Makes** :4 servings

Ingredients

- 1 package (16 ounces) potato gnocchi
- 1 pound ground chicken
- 1/2 cup chopped onion
- 2 tablespoons olive oil
- 1 jar (26 ounces) spaghetti sauce
- 1/4 teaspoon salt
- 1/4 to 1/2 teaspoon dried oregano
- Shredded Parmesan cheese, optional

Directions

1. Cook gnocchi according to package directions. Meanwhile, in a large skillet, cook chicken and onion in oil over medium heat until chicken is no longer pink; drain if necessary. Stir in the spaghetti sauce, salt and oregano; cook until heated through, 5-10 minutes.
2. Drain gnocchi; gently stir into skillet. Garnish servings with cheese if desired.

Nutrition Facts

1-1/2 cups (calculated without cheese): 598 calories, 24g fat (6g saturated fat), 88mg cholesterol, 1632mg sodium, 66g carbohydrate (19g sugars, 6g fiber), 30g protein.

Salsa Corn Cakes

Total Time:Prep/Total time: 20 min**Makes** :8 servings

Ingredients

- 6 ounces cream cheese, softened
- 1/4 cup butter, melted
- 6 large eggs
- 1 cup 2% milk
- 1-1/2 cups all-purpose flour
- 1/2 cup cornmeal
- 1 teaspoon baking powder
- 1 teaspoon salt
- 1 can (15-1/4 ounces) whole kernel corn, drained
- 1/2 cup salsa, drained
- 1/4 cup minced green onions
- Sour cream and additional salsa

Directions

1. In a large bowl, beat cream cheese and butter until smooth; add the eggs and mix well. Beat in the milk until smooth. Combine the flour, cornmeal, baking powder and salt; stir into cream cheese mixture just until moistened. Fold in the corn, salsa and onions.
2. Pour batter by 1/4 cupfuls into a large greased cast-iron skillet or hot griddle. Turn when bubbles form on top; cook until the second side is golden brown. Serve with sour cream and salsa.

Nutrition Facts

1 serving: 324 calories, 15g fat (8g saturated fat), 191mg cholesterol, 715mg sodium, 34g carbohydrate (5 sugars, 3g fiber), 11g protein.

Hash Brown Pork Skillet

Total Time:Prep/Total time: 25 min**Makes** :6 servings

Ingredients

- 4 cups frozen O'Brien potatoes, thawed
- 1 cup chopped onion
- 1 cup chopped green pepper
- 2 tablespoons butter
- 2 cups shredded cooked pork
- 2 teaspoons chicken bouillon granules
- 1/4 teaspoon pepper
- 2 teaspoons all-purpose flour
- 1/2 cup 2% milk
- 3/4 cup shredded cheddar cheese

Directions

1. In a large cast-iron or other heavy skillet, cook the potatoes, onion and green pepper in butter over medium heat until almost tender. Stir in the pork, bouillon and pepper; heat through.
2. In a small bowl, combine flour and milk until smooth; add to skillet. Cook on medium-low heat until mixture is thickened, stirring frequently, 4-5 minutes.
3. Sprinkle with cheese. Remove from the heat; cover and let stand until cheese is melted.

Nutrition Facts

1 cup: 286 calories, 13g fat (7g saturated fat), 70mg cholesterol, 449mg sodium, 22g carbohydrate (4g sugars, 3g fiber), 19g protein.

Chocolate Pecan Skillet Cookie

Total Time: Prep: 15 min Bake: 35 min.Makes :12 servings

Ingredients

- 1 cup butter
- 1 cup sugar
- 1 cup packed brown sugar
- 2 large eggs, room temperature
- 2 teaspoons vanilla extract
- 3 cups all-purpose flour
- 1-1/2 teaspoons baking soda
- 1/2 teaspoon kosher salt
- 1 cup 60% cacao bittersweet chocolate baking chips
- 1 cup chopped pecans, toasted
- Vanilla ice cream, optional

Directions

1. Preheat oven to 350°. In a 12-in. cast-iron skillet, heat butter in oven as it preheats. Meanwhile, in a large bowl, stir together sugar and brown sugar. When butter is almost melted, remove skillet from oven and swirl butter until completely melted. Stir butter into sugar mixture; set skillet aside.
2. Beat eggs and vanilla into sugar mixture. In another bowl, whisk together flour, baking soda and salt; gradually beat into sugar mixture. Stir in chocolate chips and nuts. Spread mixture into buttered skillet.
3. Bake until toothpick inserted in center comes out with moist crumbs and top is golden brown, 35-40 minutes. Serve warm, with vanilla ice cream if desired.

Test Kitchen tips

1. This cookie may be prepared in four 6-in. cast-iron skillets. Just brush skillets with melted butter before adding dough. Bake 25-30 minutes.
2. For a dairy-free option, substitute shortening or nondairy margarine for the butter.

Nutrition Facts

1 serving: 528 calories, 27g fat (13g saturated fat), 72mg cholesterol, 378mg sodium, 69g carbohydrate (43g sugars, 3g fiber), 6g protein.

Beef Skillet Supper

Total Time:Prep/Total time: 30 minMakes :8 servings

Ingredients

- 8 ounces uncooked medium egg noodles (about 4 cups)
- 1-1/2 pounds ground beef
- 1 medium onion, chopped
- 1/2 teaspoon salt
- 1/4 teaspoon pepper
- 1 can (8 ounces) tomato sauce
- 1/2 cup water
- 1 can (11 ounces) Mexicorn, drained
- 1 cup shredded cheddar cheese

Directions

1. Cook noodles according to package directions; drain.
2. Meanwhile, in a large skillet, cook and crumble beef with onion over medium-high heat until no longer pink, 6-8 minutes. Stir in salt, pepper, tomato sauce and water; bring to a boil. Reduce heat; simmer, covered, 10 minutes.

3. Stir in corn and noodles; heat through. Sprinkle with cheese; let stand, covered, until cheese is melted.

Nutrition Facts

1 serving: 368 calories, 16g fat (7g saturated fat), 90mg cholesterol, 548mg sodium, 30g carbohydrate (4g sugars, 2g fiber), 24g protein.

One-Skillet Pork Chop Supper

Total Time: **Prep**: 10 min **Bake**: 30 min.**Makes** :4 servings

Ingredients

- 1 tablespoon butter
- 4 pork loin chops (1/2 inch thick and 7 ounces each)
- 3 medium red potatoes, cut into small wedges
- 3 medium carrots, cut into 1/2-inch slices, or 2 cups fresh baby carrots
- 1 medium onion, cut into wedges
- 1 can (10-3/4 ounces) condensed cream of mushroom soup, undiluted
- 1/4 cup water
- Optional: cracked black pepper and chopped fresh parsley

Directions

1. In a large cast-iron or other heavy skillet, heat butter over medium heat. Brown pork chops on both sides; remove from pan, reserving drippings.
2. In same pan, saute vegetables in drippings until lightly browned. Whisk together soup and water; stir into vegetables. Bring to a boil. Reduce heat; simmer, covered, just until vegetables are tender, 15-20 minutes.
3. Add chops; cook, covered, until a thermometer inserted in pork reads 145°. Remove from heat; let stan 5 minutes. If desired, sprinkle with pepper and parsley.

Nutrition Facts

1 serving: 390 calories, 15g fat (6g saturated fat), 97mg cholesterol, 700mg sodium, 28g carbohydrate (6g sugars, 4g fiber), 33g protein.

Potato Pan Rolls

Total Time: **Prep**: 15 min + rising **Bake**: 20 min**Makes** :16 rolls

Ingredients

- 4-1/2 to 5 cups all-purpose flour
- 3 tablespoons sugar
- 2 packages (1/4 ounce each) quick-rise yeast
- 1-1/2 teaspoons salt
- 1-1/4 cups water
- 3 tablespoons butter
- 1/2 cup mashed potatoes (without added milk and butter)
- Additional all-purpose flour

Directions

1. In a large bowl, combine 2 cups flour, sugar, yeast and salt. In a small saucepan, heat water and butter 120°-130°. Add to dry ingredients; beat until smooth. Stir in mashed potatoes and enough remaining flour to form a soft dough.
2. Turn onto a floured surface; knead until smooth and elastic, about 6-8 minutes. Cover and let rest for minutes. Divide into 16 pieces. Shape each into a ball. Place in two greased 8- or 9-in. cast-iron skille or round baking pans. Cover and let rise in a warm place until doubled, about 30 minutes.
3. Preheat oven to 400°. Sprinkle tops of rolls with additional flour. Bake until golden brown, 18-22

minutes. Remove from pans to wire racks.

Nutrition Facts

1 roll: 163 calories, 3g fat (1g saturated fat), 6mg cholesterol, 239mg sodium, 30g carbohydrate (3g sugars, 1g fiber), 4g protein.

German Apple Pancake

Total Time: **Prep**: 15 min **Bake**: 20 min.**Makes** :6 servings

Ingredients

PANCAKE:

- 3 large eggs, room temperature
- 1 cup whole milk
- 3/4 cup all-purpose flour
- 1/2 teaspoon salt
- 1/8 teaspoon ground nutmeg
- 3 tablespoons butter

TOPPING:

- 2 tart baking apples, peeled and sliced
- 3 to 4 tablespoons butter
- 2 tablespoons sugar
- Confectioners' sugar

Directions

1. Preheat a 10-in. cast-iron skillet in a 425° oven. Meanwhile, in a blender, combine the eggs, milk, flour, salt and nutmeg; cover and process until smooth.
2. Add butter to hot skillet; return to oven until butter bubbles. Pour batter into skillet. Bake, uncovered, for 20 minutes or until pancake puffs and edges are browned and crisp.
3. For topping, in a skillet, combine the apples, butter and sugar; cook and stir over medium heat until apples are tender. Spoon into baked pancake. Sprinkle with confectioners' sugar. Cut and serve immediately.

Test Kitchen tips

1. Many fruits can be used in place of the apples. Pears, berries, peaches or plums are all delish. If you use berries, just skip the precooking step.
2. For extra flavor, try adding a splash of almond or vanilla extract to the batter.

Nutrition Facts

1 serving: 192 calories, 12g fat (7g saturated fat), 107mg cholesterol, 273mg sodium, 18g carbohydrate (8g sugars, 1g fiber), 5g protein.

Homey Mac & Cheese

Total Time: **Prep**: 20 min **Bake**: 25 min.**Makes** :8 servings

Ingredients

- 2-1/2 cups uncooked elbow macaroni
- 1/4 cup butter, cubed
- 1/4 cup all-purpose flour
- 1/2 teaspoon salt
- 1/4 teaspoon pepper
- 3 cups 2% milk
- 5 cups shredded sharp cheddar cheese, divided

- 2 tablespoons Worcestershire sauce
- 1/2 teaspoon paprika

Directions
1. Preheat oven to 350°. Cook macaroni according to package directions for al dente.
2. Meanwhile, in a large saucepan, heat butter over medium heat. Stir in flour, salt and pepper until smooth; gradually whisk in milk. Bring to a boil, stirring constantly; cook and stir until thickened, 2-3 minutes.
3. Reduce heat. Stir in 3 cups cheese and Worcestershire sauce until cheese is melted.
4. Drain macaroni; stir into sauce. Transfer to a greased 10-in. ovenproof skillet. Bake, uncovered, 20 minutes. Top with remaining cheese; sprinkle with paprika. Bake until bubbly and cheese is melted, 5-10 minutes.

Nutrition Facts
1 cup: 447 calories, 28g fat (20g saturated fat), 97mg cholesterol, 701mg sodium, 28g carbohydrate (6g sugars, 1g fiber), 22g protein.

Macaroon-Topped Rhubarb Cobbler
Total Time:Prep/Total time: 30 minMakes :4 servings

Ingredients
- 4 cups sliced fresh or frozen rhubarb (1-inch pieces)
- 1 large apple, peeled and sliced
- 1/2 cup packed brown sugar
- 1/2 teaspoon ground cinnamon, divided
- 1 tablespoon cornstarch
- 2 tablespoons cold water
- 8 macaroons, crumbled
- 1 tablespoon butter, melted
- 2 tablespoons sugar
- Vanilla ice cream, optional

Directions
1. In a large cast-iron or other ovenproof skillet, combine the rhubarb, apple, brown sugar and 1/4 teaspo cinnamon; bring to a boil. Reduce heat; cover and simmer until rhubarb is very tender, 10-13 minutes. Combine cornstarch and water until smooth; gradually add to the fruit mixture. Bring to a boil; cook a stir until thickened, about 2 minutes.
2. In a small bowl, combine the crumbled cookies, butter, sugar and remaining cinnamon. Sprinkle over fruit mixture.
3. Broil 4 in. from the heat until lightly browned, 3-5 minutes. If desired, serve warm with ice cream.

Nutrition Facts
1 serving: 368 calories, 12g fat (7g saturated fat), 8mg cholesterol, 45mg sodium, 62g carbohydrate (55g sugars, 5g fiber), 3g protein.

Honey Walleye
Total Time:Prep/Total time: 20 minMakes :6 servings

Ingredients
- 1 large egg
- 2 teaspoons honey
- 2 cups crushed Ritz crackers (about 45 to 50)

- 1/2 teaspoon salt
- 1-1/2 pounds walleye fillets
- 1/3 to 1/2 cup canola oil
- Optional: Minced fresh parsley and lemon wedges

Directions

1. In a shallow bowl, beat egg; add honey. In a shallow dish, combine crackers and salt. Dip fish in egg mixture, then in cracker mixture; turn until coated.
2. In a cast-iron or other heavy skillet, cook fillets in oil over medium heat until golden and fish flakes easily with a fork, 3-5 minutes on each side. If desired, top with parsley and serve with lemon wedges.

Nutrition Facts

3 ounces cooked fish: 389 calories, 22g fat (3g saturated fat), 133mg cholesterol, 514mg sodium, 23g carbohydrate (5g sugars, 1g fiber), 25g protein.

Chicken Burrito Skillet

Total Time: **Prep**: 15 min **Bake**: 35 min.**Makes** :6 servings

Ingredients

- 1 pound boneless skinless chicken breasts, cut into 1-1/2-inch pieces
- 1/8 teaspoon salt
- 1/8 teaspoon pepper
- 2 tablespoons olive oil, divided
- 1 cup uncooked long grain rice
- 1 can (15 ounces) black beans, rinsed and drained
- 1 can (14-1/2 ounces) diced tomatoes, drained
- 1 teaspoon ground cumin
- 1/2 teaspoon onion powder
- 1/2 teaspoon garlic powder
- 1/2 teaspoon chili powder
- 2-1/2 cups reduced-sodium chicken broth
- 1 cup shredded Mexican cheese blend
- 1 medium tomato, chopped
- 3 green onions, chopped

Directions

1. Toss chicken with salt and pepper. In a large cast-iron or other heavy skillet, heat 1 tablespoon oil over medium-high heat; saute chicken until browned, about 2 minutes. Remove from pan.
2. In same pan, heat remaining oil over medium-high heat; saute rice until lightly browned, 1-2 minutes. Stir in beans, canned tomatoes, seasonings and broth; bring to a boil. Place chicken on top (do not stir into rice). Simmer, covered, until rice is tender and chicken is no longer pink, 20-25 minutes.
3. Remove from heat; sprinkle with cheese. Let stand, covered, until cheese is melted. Top with tomato and green onions.

Test Kitchen tips

1. Any can of beans you have in your pantry will work well in this recipe. We particularly like pintos and kidney beans here.
2. Bump up the health factor by using brown rice instead of white

Nutrition Facts

1-1/3 cups: 403 calories, 13g fat (4g saturated fat), 58mg cholesterol, 690mg sodium, 43g carbohydrate (4g sugars, 5g fiber), 27g protein. Diabetic Exchanges: 3 starch, 3 lean meat, 1-1/2 fat.

Total Time: Prep: 1 hour + chilling Bake: 65 min.+ coolingMakes : 10 servings

Ingredients

- 2-1/2 cups all-purpose flour
- 1/2 teaspoon salt
- 1-1/4 cups cold lard
- 6 to 8 tablespoons cold 2% milk

FILLING:

- 2-1/2 cups sugar
- 1 teaspoon ground cinnamon
- 1/2 teaspoon ground ginger
- 9 cups thinly sliced peeled tart apples (about 9 medium)
- 1 tablespoon bourbon, optional
- 2 tablespoons all-purpose flour
- Dash salt
- 3 tablespoons cold butter, cubed

TOPPING:

- 1 tablespoon 2% milk
- 2 teaspoons coarse sugar

Directions

1. In a large bowl, mix flour and salt; cut in lard until crumbly. Gradually add milk, tossing with a fork until dough holds together when pressed. Divide dough in half. Shape each into a disk; wrap in plastic. Refrigerate 1 hour or overnight.
2. For filling, in a large bowl, mix sugar, cinnamon and ginger. Add apples and toss to coat. Cover; let stand 1 hour to allow apples to release juices, stirring occasionally.
3. Drain apples, reserving syrup. Place syrup and, if desired, bourbon in a small saucepan; bring to a boil. Reduce heat; simmer, uncovered, 20-25 minutes or until mixture thickens slightly and turns a medium amber color. Remove from heat; cool completely.
4. Preheat oven to 400°. Toss drained apples with flour and salt. On a lightly floured surface, roll one half of dough to a 1/8-in.-thick circle; transfer to a 10-in. cast-iron or other deep ovenproof skillet. Trim pastry even with rim. Add apple mixture. Pour cooled syrup over top; dot with butter.
5. Roll remaining dough to a 1/8-in.-thick circle. Place over filling. Trim, seal and flute edge. Cut slits in top. Brush milk over pastry; sprinkle with coarse sugar. Place on a foil-lined baking sheet. Bake 20 minutes.
6. Reduce oven setting to 350°. Bake 45-55 minutes longer or until crust is golden brown and filling is bubbly. Cool on a wire rack.

Nutrition Facts

1 piece: 633 calories, 30g fat (12g saturated fat), 34mg cholesterol, 169mg sodium, 90g carbohydrate (62g sugars, 2g fiber), 4g protein.

SERVES: 2 TO 10   PREP TIME: 10 MINS   COOK TIME: 40 MINS

Ingredients

- Small red bliss, yukon gold, or other waxy potatoes, 1 1/2 to 2 inches in size
- Olive oil
- Kosher salt (I prefer Morton Kosher salt here as it is more coarse than Diamond Crystal)

Directions

1. Halve the potatoes and place the cut side down; halve each half again but keep these halves together.
2. Choose a cast iron skillet large enough to accommodate the halved potatoes. Add enough olive oil to coat the bottom of the pan 1/8 inch deep in oil. Heat the oil over medium heat until it begins to shimmer. Sprinkle a generous layer of salt into the oil all over the bottom of the pan, as evenly as possible in a thin layer. Place the potato halves onto the salt (keeping the pieces of second cut together so the potatoes look like just one half). Fry at medium heat (without peeking) until you are sure that the potatoes must be burning (they're not!), about 10 to 12 minutes depending on the size of the potatoes. At 10 minutes, gently turn over a potato half to see if it is nicely browned; if not, continue cooking a few more minutes.
3. When the potatoes are nicely browned, turn the heat as low as possible and cover the pan. You will hear spattering noises as the potatoes start to steam, and they will continue to brown under cover.
4. Cook about 20 minutes covered. The potatoes are done when a sharp knife slips into a potato easily. Serve hot. Kept covered with the heat off, they will keep for 30 minutes or more. If you are letting them stand, drain off any excess oil from the pan. They are equally good at room temperature.

Avocado Cornbread

SERVES: one 9-inch round cornbread

Ingredients

- 1 cup stone ground cornmeal
- 1/2 cup all purpose flour
- 1 1/2 teaspoons baking soda
- 1/2 teaspoon salt
- 1/2 teaspoon cayenne pepper (or more if you like spicy - I do!)
- 2 teaspoons cumin
- 6 tablespoons butter
- 2 tablespoons honey
- 1 cup buttermilk
- 1 egg
- 1 ear corn cut from the cob (about 1 1/2 cup)
- 1 large ripe avocado in 1/2" cubes (about 1 1/2 cup)
- Juice from 1/2 lime (about 2 teaspoons)

Directions

1. Heat the oven to 400. Put 2 tablespoons butter and 1 teaspoon cumin in a 9-inch iron skillet or a cake pan and stick it in the oven.
2. Whisk the remaining dry ingredients together. Melt the remaining butter and honey together (honey measuring tip - give your measuring spoon a spritz of no-stick before pouring in the honey - it will slide right out). Mix the corn and avocado - squeeze the lime over and toss gently to coat. In a large bowl - whisk together the egg and buttermilk. Yes, you have now dirtied up 4 bowls. But you can wash them while the cornbread bakes.
3. Slowly whisk the melted butter and honey into the buttermilk and egg. Next stir in the dry ingredients and then gently fold in the avocado and corn. Get the hot pan out of the oven and pour in the batter.
4. Put the cornbread back in the oven and reduce the heat to 375. Bake 30-40 minutes until it is golden brown and a tester comes out clean (unless you hit avocado!)
5. Allow to cool some before you serve.

Japanese-Style Fried Tofu

SERVES: 2-3

Ingredients

- 1 pound extra firm tofu
- 1/4 cup shiro miso paste (white miso)
- 1/4 cup ponzu sauce
- 1/4 cup dark brown sugar
- 1/4 cup honey
- 2 tablespoons rice vinegar
- 2 tablespoons mirin
- 1 1/2 teaspoons wasabi paste
- 1 1/2 tablespoons ginger paste
- 4 cloves of garlic, finely minced
- Vegetable oil, for frying

Directions

1. Gently press the block of tofu after wrapping it in paper towels. You'll see a lot of water coming out, make sure you don't press too hard as you don't want it to crumble. Once most of the moisture has been pressed out, cut into 1 1/2 inch cubes. Set aside.
2. Mix all the rest of the ingredients, except for the oil, in a glass bowl. Submerge the tofu pieces in the marinade and park it in the fridge for at least 24 hours to up to 48 hours (like I did). Give it a shake every now and then.
3. Heat a big skillet and pour enough vegetable oil to coat the bottom of the pan. On medium heat add the pieces of tofu in a single layer. Be careful, it is going to splatter like crazy!! Using tongs GENTLY turn them around and fry them on all sides. Once they are nicely browned on all sides, drain them on a paper towel.
4. You could have the tofu as it is, or you could use it with your favorite stir fry, on salads, in wraps or sandwiches. Enjoy!

Persimmon Latkes

MAKES: 10 latkes

Ingredients

- 3 small yellow potatoes (about 12 oz)
- 2 firm Fuyu persimmons (about 9oz)
- 2 eggs, lightly beaten
- 1 small garlic clove, mashed
- 1 pinch cumin (1/4 teaspoon or less)
- 1 pinch nutmeg
- Salt and pepper
- Oil, for frying

Directions

1. Peel the potatoes and grate them coarsely, by hand or in a food processor. Let the potatoes rest for a couple of minutes and then squeeze excess water by hand. Reserve the water in a small bowl and leave for about 15 minutes. After 15 minutes, pour off all the liquid from the bowl, but leave the white potato starch that settled on the bottom.
2. Grate the persimmons (without peeling them).
3. In a large bowl, mix the potatoes, persimmons, starch, eggs, cumin, nutmeg, garlic, salt and pepper.
4. In a large skillet heat the oil over moderately high heat until hot but not smoking. Spoon about 1 1/2 tablespoons of mixture per latke into the skillet, spreading into flat rounds with a fork. (Do not overcrowd the skillet.) Reduce heat to medium and fry the latkes until undersides are dark golden, about four to five minutes. Using a spatula carefully turn the latkes over (be gentle as there is no flour in the mixture and they will be prone to breaking easily) and fry until undersides are dark golden, about four

five minutes more. Transfer the latkes to paper towels to drain. Serve immediately.

Charlotte Druckman's Olive (Oil) Cake

PREP TIME: 10 minutes **COOK TIME**: 30 minutes **MAKES**one 9- or 10-inch cake

Ingredients

- 3/4 cup (95g) all-purpose flour
- 1/4 cup (25g) almond meal
- 1 teaspoon baking powder (the aluminum-free kind, if you can find it)
- 1/8 teaspoon fine salt
- 1/2 cup (100g) light or dark brown sugar
- 1/2 cup (100g) granulated sugar, divided
- 1/2 cup (110g) extra-virgin olive oil
- 2 large eggs
- 1 tablespoon vanilla extract
- 5/8 cup (80g) pitted oil-cured black olives, roughly chopped

Directions

1. Heat the oven to 350°F with a well-seasoned 10-inch cast-iron skillet in it. (9-inch is fine if that's what you have—it will just take a little longer to bake.)
2. Sift or whisk together the flour, baking powder, and salt in a medium bowl. In the bowl of a stand mixer (or using a large mixing bowl and handheld electric mixer), beat the olive oil, brown sugar, and 1/4 cup + 2 tablespoons (75g) granulated sugar together on medium-high speed until thoroughly combined. Add the eggs, one at a time, to incorporate, scraping down the bowl, then add the vanilla and beat to incorporate.
3. Decrease the speed to low and add the dry ingredients, mixing until just combined.
4. Remove the hot cast-iron skillet from the oven and carefully brush the bottom and sides with olive oil. Scrape the batter into the skillet and smooth the top. Scatter the olives all over the batter, covering it. Sprinkle the top evenly with the remaining 2 tablespoons sugar (25g). Remembering the pan and handle are hot (!), return it to the oven.
5. Bake until cake is golden and a toothpick inserted into a center part of the cake comes out free of batter, about 30 to 40 minutes.
6. Wait a good 10 minutes before flipping the cake out of the skillet. Use a butter or dinner knife (not too sharp) to make sure the cake is loosened from the sides of the pan, and, if necessary, to coax the edges off the bottom of the pan for easy flipping. Have two plates ready, because you'll need to flip it twice so it's right (olive) side up.
7. Depending on how well-seasoned your cast iron pan is, it's possible that the bottom will stick. If it's sticking all over, let it cool and firm up a bit more, then try to ease it out with a spatula, or just serve it from the pan. If one spot sticks and remains in the pan after you flip out, tuck the missing piece in like a puzzle and no one will notice! Let cake cool completely before serving.

Dark Chocolate-Olive Oil Skillet Banana Bread

SERVES at least 8

Ingredients

- 1 1/2 cups (180g) unbleached all-purpose flour
- 1/2 cup (43g) unsweetened cocoa (regular or Dutch-process)
- 3/4 cup (140g) dark brown sugar
- 3/4 teaspoon baking soda
- 3/4 teaspoon sea salt or kosher salt

- 1/3 cup (80ml) extra-virgin olive oil
- 2 large eggs, lightly beaten
- 1 1/2 cups (350g) ultra ripe bananas (from about 3 large bananas), mashed with a fork into a smooth puree
- 1/4 cup (60g) sour cream or plain Greek yogurt (full fat is best)
- 1 1/2 teaspoons vanilla extract
- 1 cup (113g) coarsely chopped dark chocolate (equals a 4-ounce bar), or an equal amount of dark chocolate chips
- 1/2 cup (65g) chopped pecans or walnuts (optional)

Directions

1. Preheat the oven to 350° F. Generously butter or grease with olive oil a 10-inch enameled or well-seasoned cast-iron skillet, or a 9x5-inch loaf pan. (If your skillet isn't well-seasoned, you can line the bottom with a round of parchment paper.)
2. In a large bowl, whisk together the flour, cocoa, brown sugar, baking soda, and salt.
3. In a separate bowl, mix together the olive oil, eggs, mashed banana, sour cream, and vanilla. Pour the banana mixture into the flour mixture and fold with a spatula until just combined. Fold in the chocolate and pecans (if using), again just until combined. Scrape the batter into the prepared skillet.
4. Bake until golden brown and a toothpick or knife inserted into the center of the bread comes out clear, about 28 to 35 minutes (start checking at about 22 minutes for doneness). Let cool in skillet for about to 30 minutes, and serve warm or at room temperature, straight from the pan. (If using a loaf pan, the baking time will be closer to 55 to 65 minutes. Let cool in the loaf pan for about 10 to 15 minutes, the run a knife around the edge of the pan and invert it onto a cooling rack.)

Dutch Baby with Orange Sugar

PREP TIME10 Min TOTAL TIME 30 Min SERVES 6 - 8

Ingredients

- ⅓ cup sugar
- 1 well-scrubed orange, zested
- 3 large eggs, at room temperature
- ⅔ cup whole milk, at room temperature
- ⅔ cup all-purpose flour
- ½ tsp pure vanilla extract
- ¼ tsp cinnamon
- ¼ tsp ground nutmeg
- ¼ tsp salt
- 5 Tbsp (about 1/2 stick) unsalted butter, cut into pieces

Directions

1. Put skillet on middle rack of oven and preheat to 450°F.
2. Stir together sugar and zest in a small bowl and set aside.
3. Beat eggs with an electric mixer at high speed until pale and frothy, then add the milk, flour, vanilla, cinnamon, nutmeg, and salt and continue to beat for about one minute.
4. Add butter to the hot skillet and melt, swirling to coat. Add batter and immediately return skillet to oven.
5. Bake until puffed and golden-brown, 17-20 minutes.
6. Top with orange sugar and serve immediately.

Skillet Cookie Sundae

PREP TIME 15 Min TOTAL TIME 55 Min SERVES 10 - 12

Ingredients

- 2 sticks butter, softened
- 1 cup packed brown sugar
- ½ cup granulated sugar
- 1 Tbsp vanilla extract
- 2 eggs
- 2 cups all-purpose flour
- 2 heaping tsp instant coffee
- 1 ½ tsp baking soda
- 1 tsp salt
- 1 cup milk chocolate chips
- 1 cup semisweet chocolate chips
- Ice cream, such as vanilla, strawberry, mint chocolate chip or chocolate, for serving
- Hot fudge, for serving
- Canned whipped cream, for serving
- Maraschino cherries, for serving

Directions

1. Preheat the oven to 350ºF.
2. Cream together the butter, brown sugar and granulated sugar in a large bowl. Add the vanilla and eggs, mixing well. Combine the flour, instant coffee, baking soda and salt in a separate bowl. Add the dry ingredients to the wet ingredients in 3 batches, mixing after each one. Stir in the milk and semisweet chocolate chips.
3. Spread the mixture into a 10-inch skillet and bake until golden brown, 30 to 40 minutes. Remove the skillet from the oven, top the cookie with several scoops of your favorite ice cream, drizzle on some hot fudge and top with whipped cream and a cherry.

Skillet Chicken Lasagna

PREP TIME 10 Min TOTAL TIME 40 Min SERVES 8

Ingredients

- 12 oz bow tie pasta
- 2 Tbsp olive oil
- 2 skinless, boneless chicken breasts, sliced or diced
- 1 Tbsp Italian seasoning, or herbes de Provence
- Salt
- 1 medium onion, diced
- 2 cloves garlic, minced
- 1 cup low-sodium chicken broth
- 1 jar marinara sauce, good-quality (14 to 16 oz)
- 1 tsp red pepper flakes
- 1 cup grated mozzarella cheese, plus more if needed
- ½ cup whole milk ricotta cheese, plus more if needed
- ¼ cup grated Parmesan, plus more if needed and for serving
- 12 fresh basil leaves, cut into chiffonade or chopped, plus more if needed and for serving

Directions

1. Cook the pasta according to the package instructions; drain and set aside.
2. Heat the oil in a large skillet over medium-high heat. Season the chicken with the Italian seasoning and some salt. Add the chicken to the skillet and cook until golden brown, 2 to 3 minutes per side. Remove the chicken to a plate and set aside.

3. Add the onions and garlic to the same skillet and cook, stirring, for 3 minutes. Add the broth, then scrape the bottom of the skillet to loosen the bits. Cook for another 2 to 3 minutes to let the broth reduce. Add the marinara sauce and red pepper flakes, bring to a simmer and simmer for 10 minutes.
4. Turn off the heat and add the drained pasta, mozzarella, ricotta, Parmesan and basil. Add the cooked chicken on top. Toss to combine, then add more of the mozzarella, ricotta, Parmesan or basil until the sauce is just how you like it. Serve with a sprinkling of Parmesan and a little basil on top.

Cast Iron Berry Cobbler

PREP TIME 10 Min TOTAL TIME 45 Min SERVES 6

Ingredients

- 1 ½ cups (325 mL) blackberries
- 2 cups (500 mL) blueberries
- 6 cups (1.5 L) strawberries, sliced
- 2 Tbsp (30 mL) sugar
- ½ cup (125 mL) flour
- 1 cup (250 mL) quick oats
- ¼ cup (60 mL) brown sugar
- ⅓ cup (90 mL) cold butter, cubed

Directions

1. Preheat grill to 350ºF.
2. Stir berries with sugar in a large bowl. Pour into a cast iron pan.
3. Combine flour with oats, brown sugar and butter in a medium bowl. Rub mixture together until ingredients are coated with butter and mixture resembles a crumble topping. Sprinkle over fruit.
4. Transfer pan to the grill and cook with the lid down for 35 to 40 minutes or until top is golden and mixture is bubbling. Remove from grill and allow to cool for 20 minutes. Spoon warm cobbler over ice cream.